ARISE
AND GO

Kevin Connolly grew up in Bailieborough, Co. Cavan, where, among the drumlins, he discovered the poetry of W.B. Yeats. He opened The Winding Stair Bookshop and Café on Dublin's quays in 1982, which he owned until 2006. He lives in Co. Sligo.

ARISE
AND GO
W.B.YEATS

AND THE PEOPLE AND PLACES
THAT INSPIRED HIM

Kevin Connolly

THE O'BRIEN PRESS
DUBLIN

Dedication

To my father, Brian,
and in memory of my mother, Marguerite, with love
'"F" is for ceiling'
and in memory of Philip Casey, friend.

Acknowledgments

The author would like to thank the following for their presence, patience
and friendship: Tim and Janet, Terry and Sally, Ken and Deb, Barb H,
Elaine, Chris and Beryl, Naomi and Mark, Aideen, Melissa and Gail, Laura
and Gary, Mona and Niall, Almut, Connie and Jim, Liz and Tom KR,
Don and Cath, Anto and Adi, All at IRC, and Patsy, Anne, Michael, Sean,
Eileen, and Brendan Connolly, Linda, Don, Erica, Nolan, and especially
Heidi Fledderjohn and Danny, and Murph, dear companion and friend.

He would particularly like to thank Nicola Reddy at The O'Brien Press for
her commitment, dedication, and expert guidance throughout this project.
With special thanks to Benedict and Leila.

ARISE
AND GO

First published 2024 by The O'Brien Press Ltd,
12 Terenure Road East, Rathgar, Dublin 6, D06 HD27, Ireland.
Tel: +353 1 4923333; Fax: +353 1 4922777
Email: books@obrien.ie; Website: obrien.ie.
Originally published in hardback 2019.
Parts of the Sligo chapter based on *Yeats and Sligo* by Kevin Connolly,
published 2010 by Brandon, an imprint of Mount Eagle Publications.
The O'Brien Press is a member of Publishing Ireland.

ISBN: 978-1-78849-485-4

7 6 5 4 3 2 1
28 27 26 25 24

Printed and bound in Poland by Bialostockie Zaklady Graficzne S.A.
The paper in this book is produced using pulp from managed forests.

Great Irish books
O'BRIEN
obrien.ie

Published in
DUBLIN
UNESCO
City of Literature

CONTENTS

INTRODUCTION

I call on those that call me son,
Grandson, or great-grandson,
On uncles, aunts, great-uncles or great-aunts,
To judge what I have done.
Have I, that put it into words,
Spoilt what old loins have sent?

– from 'Are You Content' (*New Poems*, 1938)

The profound influence of place runs like a river through the life and works of the poet and playwright W.B. Yeats. From his birthplace in Dublin to his final resting place in Sligo, we can trace the arc of Yeats's awakening as man and poet, see the emerging creative being within him as he learns, and then hones, his craft. This book does not claim to be a full chronicle of his life's journey; there is no mention of his time in France other than his death, nor in Italy with Ezra Pound, nor his trips to the United States, nor his time in Oxford. Rather, it focuses on his time in Dublin, London, Sligo and elsewhere in the west of Ireland, embracing many of the main points and people that impacted his life and stimulated his vast body of work.

In his unsettled childhood, Yeats alternated between the anonymity of London, where the family struggled with financial insecurity, and Dublin, where they occupied a twilight zone between middle-class aspirations and an uncomfortable bohemianism, and his beloved Sligo, with his mother's family, where they were 'somebodys' with the respect and station earned by the commercial endeavours of the Pollexfen and Middleton families. Here the young Yeatses were allowed to roam and flourish, listening to the unworldly tales of house servants and fishermen, cloaked by the mists of Celtic mythology and folklore. Here, too, was the landscape of W.B. Yeats's poetic imagination, rich with legend and imagery, filled with the voices of the peasantry and the music of the hills and the sea.

Then on to the suburbs of London, to Howth and the Georgian squares of Dublin, the Abbey Theatre and its Celtic revival, to Glendalough, the wilds of County Galway and Coole Park, Thoor Ballylee, Frenchpark, Lough Key in Roscommon, and, ultimately, to Sligo, Yeats's land of heart's desire, where was sowed, in that sensitive and creative mind, the seeds of the muse that was to sustain his poetic endeavours for the remainder of his life.

These landscapes, both real and imagined, were the settings of Yeats's philosophical and literary inspiration, surrounded and witnessed by family, friends, artists and writers, and by the many other men and women who filled his days and flooded his world with ideas, with challenges, with passion and love. Meet the poet's father, the artist John Butler Yeats, who turned his back on a promising legal career to immerse himself in the pursuit of a life as an artist while enduring financial hardship. His mother, Susan, the well-to-do Sligo girl who had no choice but to follow her husband's path; who would eventually drift away from the people and places she had known and loved as a child. Their six children: the poet Willie; Lily and

Where the wandering
water gushes:
Glencar Waterfall, Leitrim

Lolly, guiding lights in the Irish Arts and Crafts movement of the early twentieth century; Jack, the renowned painter; and Bobbie and Jane Grace, who died in infancy. Meet William Morris, John O'Leary, Katharine Tynan, Madame Blavatsky, George Moore, Oscar Wilde, Lady Gregory, Douglas Hyde, George Hyde-Lees and, of course, Maud Gonne, as well as countless others who helped embroider the cloth of Yeats's poetic gift.

Lough Gill

DUBLIN

Howth: a view of the Baily Lighthouse,
with Ireland's Eye in the distance

Come near, come near, come near – Ah, leave me still
A little space for the rose-breath to fill!
Lest I no more hear common things that crave;
The weak worm hiding down in its small cave,
The field-mouse running by me in the grass,
And heavy mortal hopes that toil and pass;
But seek alone to hear the strange things said
By God to the bright hearts of those long dead,
And learn to chaunt a tongue men do not know.
Come near; I would, before my time to go,
Sing of old Eire and the ancient ways:
Red Rose, proud Rose, sad Rose of all my days.

– from 'To the Rose upon the Rood of Time'
(*Poems*, 1895)

W.B. Yeats's birthplace, Georgeville on Sandymount Avenue, and the poet as a baby

The poet William Butler Yeats was born on June 13th, 1865, at a two-storey semi-detached brick house called Georgeville at 5 Sandymount Avenue, Dublin. This was the first home that the poet's parents, John Butler Yeats (JBY) and Susan Pollexfen, shared after they were married in St. John's Church of Ireland church in Sligo, in 1863. JBY, twenty-four years old at that time, was still pursuing a career as a barrister that seemed to promise all the respectability and, more importantly, the financial and social security that Susan's successful Sligo business family desired and expected for their daughter. In January of 1866 he was indeed called to the Irish Bar. However, by the spring of 1867, with a second child, Susan Mary (Lily), and much to the consternation of the Pollexfens, John Butler Yeats had given up the law and decided instead to become an artist. With this decision began JBY's life of impecuniousness that was to exasperate those who knew and admired him, no one so much as his wife.

The Yeats family already had a connection to Sandymount through the poet's grandfather, also named William Butler Yeats, whose brother-in-law Robert Corbet was then a successful stockbroker and a representative for the Royal Exchange Assurance Company. The Corbets lived in Sandymount Castle, an eighteenth-century turreted mansion to which battlements, a clock-tower and other neo-Gothic modifications had been added. Now absorbed into the south Dublin suburb and overlooking the village green, in Yeats's childhood it was still a walled, secluded estate with maintained gardens where fruit and vegetables were grown for the house. JBY, in his memoirs, describes the building and its occupants:

> *Of business [Corbet] knew little or nothing, and probably neglected it. But he did not neglect his gardens ... He employed four or five gardeners, and as long as I knew Sandymount Castle none of these men ever left him and no one interfered with them. So treated, they were gentle, pleasant and diligent, and the gardens were lovely. There was a piece of water called the 'pond' on which we boys did much boating, and there were plenty of wild ducks and swans, and there was also an island on which was a one-roomed cottage in which was a collection of souvenirs and relics brought back from India and the Colonies by my uncle's brothers who had been soldiers. Outside the cottage were two chained eagles.*
> – *Early Memories* by John Butler Yeats, 1923

William Butler Yeats, the poet's grandfather, retired to a pretty house on the estate that was separated from the castle grounds by a wicket gate. This house later became a Presbyterian college.

Robert Corbet's own story ended tragically when, in 1870 and mired in bankruptcy, he threw himself into the Irish Sea from the Holyhead mailboat. On his death the house was sold, and the eagles were donated to the Zoological Gardens.

* * *

In 1867, when W.B. Yeats was two, he, his mother and sister Lily followed JBY to London to support him in his efforts to become a successful artist. Willie's childhood was spent between London and Sligo, where they would stay with Susan's relations, the Pollexfens and Middletons. Then in the summer of 1881, John Butler Yeats's precarious financial circumstances forced the family to return to Dublin. He believed he could get work as an artist and found a studio to rent at 44 York Street, just off St. Stephen's Green. The family were able to stay at a cottage in Howth, then a small fishing village at the northern end of Dublin Bay. (Younger brother Jack stayed on in Sligo.) Balscadden House is a long, high-walled cottage on Balscadden Road with views across Howth Harbour towards Ireland's Eye, a small island just off the coast. The sixteen-year-old described the family's new lodgings:

Our house for the first year or so was at the top of a cliff, so that in stormy weather the spray would soak my bed at night, for I had taken the glass out of the window, sash and all. Then for another year or two, we had a house overlooking the harbour where the one great sight was the going and coming of the fishing fleet.
– Reveries, *1915*

In the spring of 1882, no doubt escaping the ravages of the sea at Balscadden House, which had been intended as a summer holiday home for its owners, the Yeatses moved down to Island View on the Harbour Road. Susan felt at home among the people of Howth, who reminded her of those of her youth in Sligo, as Yeats reveals in *Reveries*:

I have no doubt that we lived at the harbour for my mother's sake ... When I think of her, I almost always see her talking over a cup of tea in the kitchen with our servant, the fisherman's wife, on the only theme out-side our house that seemed of interest – the fishing people of Howth, or the pilots and fishing people of Rosses Point. She read no books, but she and the fisherman's wife would tell each other stories that Homer might have told, pleased with any moment of sudden intensity and laughing together over any point of satire.

In his essay 'Village Ghosts' (*The Celtic Twilight*, 1893), Yeats investigates the streets and ghostly lore of Howth:

My ghosts inhabit the village of H—, in Leinster. History has in no manner been burdened by this ancient village, with its crooked lanes, its old abbey churchyard full of long grass, its green background of small fir-trees, and its quay, where lie a few tarry fishing-luggers. In the annals of entomology it is well known. For a small bay lies westward a little, where he who watches night after night may see a certain rare moth fluttering along the edge of the tide, just at the end of evening or the beginning of dawn. A hundred years ago it was carried here from Italy by smugglers in a cargo of silks and laces. If the moth-hunter would throw down his net, and go hunting for ghost tales or tales of those children of Lilith we call faeries, he would have need for far less patience.

… These H— spirits have a gloomy, matter of fact way with them. They come to announce a death, to fulfill some obligation, to revenge a wrong, to pay their bills even – as did a fisherman's daughter the other day – and then hasten to their rest … In the western tales is a whimsical grace, a curious extravagance. The people who recount them live in the most wild and beautiful scenery, under a sky ever loaded and fantastic with flying clouds.

The Yeatses' home 'at the
top of a cliff', Balscadden
House in Howth

In the wild and rugged hills of Howth, as in Sligo, the teenage Yeats found plenty to stir his awakening imagination. Among the raths, the heather and the caves, with the clamouring accompaniment of sucking tides and the high-pitched call of seabirds, Yeats created his own world, peopled by faeries and spirits, ghosts and legendary beings whose mention had instilled in him the same fascination he had felt in Sligo, listening to those who worked the land and sea and whose conversation was brimming with rich tales of mystery and other-worldliness.

Howth was also redolent with echoes of Celtic myth and legend. Ireland's Eye, the island visible slightly to the north and east of the village, is considered to be the Innisfallen in Ossian's tale, where the blessed abbot walked two hundred years about the island that wasn't a mile around. On the grounds of Howth Castle is an ancient stone grave that is said to be the place where Diarmuid and Grainne first rested on their journey of escape from Finn that ended on the slopes of Ben Bulben in Sligo. Ranging over the headlands and up to Howth Castle on paths teeming with rhododendron bushes, Yeats created his own narrative, gathering local knowledge from the seamen and herdsmen and collecting butterflies and moths and other insects in boxes.

A herd had shown me a cave some hundred and fifty feet below the cliff path and a couple of hundred above the sea, and told me that an evicted tenant called Macrom, dead some fifteen years, had lived there many years ... Here I stored a tin of cocoa and some biscuits, and instead of going to my bed, would slip out on warm nights and sleep in the cave on the excuse of catching moths. One had to pass over a rocky ledge, safe enough for any one with a fair head, yet seeming, if looked at from above, narrow and sloping; and a remonstrance from a stranger who had seen me climbing along it doubled my delight in the adventure. When, however, upon a bank holiday, I found lovers in my cave, I was not content with it again till I heard that the ghost of Macrom had been seen a little before the dawn, stooping over his fire in the cave-mouth ... At other times I would sleep among the rhododendrons and rocks in the wilder part of the grounds of Howth Castle.

 – Reveries, 1915

Howth was also the place of Yeats's sexual awakening and where he met the first love of his life, a distant cousin named Laura Armstrong, related to him through the Corbet family of Sandymount.

It all came upon me when I was close upon seventeen like the bursting of a shell ... As I look backward, I seem to discover that my passions, my loves, and my despairs, instead of being my enemies, a disturbance and an attack, became so beautiful that I had to be constantly alone to give them my whole attention.

 ... I was climbing up a hill at Howth when I heard wheels behind me and a pony-carriage drew up beside me. A pretty girl was driving alone and without a hat. She told me her name and said we had friends in common and asked me to ride beside her. After that I saw a great deal of her and was soon in love. I did not tell her I was in love, however, because she was engaged. She had chosen me for her confidant and I learned all about her quarrels with her lover ... I wrote her some bad poems and had more than one sleepless night through anger with her betrothed.

 – Reveries, 1915

Though Laura was three years older than Yeats, the young poet was entranced by her wild spirit, her buoyant nature and her skill at mimicry. In addition to the 'bad poems' he wrote for her, he also saw her as the model for the female heroines in some of his early plays.

Laura Armstrong caused Yeats a good deal of romantic uncertainty at this time, and her on-off engagement and willingness to confide in the adolescent Yeats confused him. Though we have come to recognise the pre-eminence of Maud Gonne when considering Yeats's love interests – and though he had, by this time, already met Gonne for the first time in London – it is interesting to note that, in a letter to his good friend Katharine Tynan, he writes that …

… she interests me far more than Miss Gonne does and yet is only as a myth and a symbol. I heard from her about two years ago and am trying to find out where she is now in order to send her 'Oisin'. 'Time and the Witch Vivien' was written for her to act. 'The Island of Statues' was begun with the same notion though it soon grew beyond the scope of drawing room acting. The part of the enchantress in both poems was written for her. She used to sign her letters Vivien.
– Letters Volume 1, 1889

However, and to Yeats's anguish, Laura was to marry a Dublin solicitor, Henry Byrne, whom she later divorced.

But if Howth was the setting for Yeats's first romantic aspirations, it was not by any means the last time that this craggy peninsula would witness the poet's declarations of love. In August 1891, he and Maud Gonne, the woman widely considered to have been the shimmering, spectral, unattainable but inspirational love of his life, went for a walk around the cliffs of Howth Head, where Maud had also lived for a few years as a child. The previous day Yeats had proposed marriage to her for the first time, but she had, as she would continue to do, declined his offer.

We spent the next day upon the cliff paths at Howth and dined at a little cottage near the Baily lighthouse, where her old nurse lived, and I overheard the old nurse asking if we were engaged to be married. At the day's end I found I had spent ten shillings, which seemed to me a very great sum.
— Autobiographies, 1927

The Howth cliff walk

Howth Harbour

During the walk Gonne announced that, if given the choice, she would be a seagull, which inspired Yeats to write 'The White Birds' over the next few days.

I would that we were, my beloved, white birds on the foam of the sea!
We tire of the flame of the meteor, before it can fade and flee;
And the flame of the blue star of twilight, hung low on the rim
of the sky,
Has awaked in our hearts, my beloved, a sadness that may not die.
A weariness comes from those dreamers, dew-dabbled, the lily and rose;
Ah, dream not of them, my beloved, the flame of the meteor that goes,
Or the flame of the blue star that lingers hung low in the fall of the dew:
For I would we were changed to white birds on the wandering foam:
I and you!
I am haunted by numberless islands, and many a Danaan shore,
Where Time would surely forget us, and Sorrow come near us no more;
Soon far from the rose and the lily and fret of the flames would we be,
Were we only white birds, my beloved, buoyed out on the foam of the sea!

– Poems, 1895

But W.B. Yeats's interests weren't all cerebral, literary, spiritual or romantic. He had a great love of the sea, no doubt inherited from his mother's sea-going relatives. The young Yeats was very fond of rowing and sailing, and though he had little understanding of the currents and tides of the waters around Howth, there are recorded adventures in Sligo, where he and his brother Jack were once caught in a treacherous turning tide between Rosses Point and Oyster Island.

In *Prodigal Father: The Life of John Butler Yeats* by William

M. Murphy (1978), we read of a sailing trip that Willie took with his good friend Charles Johnston.

One evening Papa was frightened when he arrived home in Howth to discover that Willie and Charlie were missing somewhere on the water in a rowboat. It was almost dark, and the boys had been gone for hours. An alarmed JBY insisted on rowing out with a fisherman, who was too polite to tell him that the boys were hopelessly lost; by the details he gave of the tides and current he left no doubt that he thought the boys had been swept out to sea. When they reached Ireland's Eye, a small rocky island about a mile from shore, they shouted but got no response. Just as JBY had almost, but not quite, lost hope they heard from the distance 'a faint halloo' and, rowing in the direction of the sound, found the boys on a point of land, without topcoats and without food. They had rowed to the island deliberately, pulled the boat back up on shore, and gone off to explore the cliffs. When they returned they found the outgoing tide had left their boat high and dry and 'immoveable'.

It was while living at Howth that W.B. Yeats began to travel with his father by early-morning train to Dublin.

My father's influence upon my thought was at its height. We went by train to Dublin every morning, breakfasting in his studio [located at] a York St. tenement house, and at breakfast he read passages from the poets, and always from the play or poem at its most passionate moment.
– Reveries, 1915

One day JBY instructed Willie to walk the five minutes to Harcourt Street and enrol at the Erasmus Smith High School.

I was now fifteen; and as he did not want to leave his painting my father told me to go to Harcourt Street and put myself to school. I found a bleak eighteenth-century house, a small playing field full of mud and pebbles, fenced by an iron railing, and opposite a long hoarding and a squalid, ornamental railway station.

– *Reveries*, 1915

The High School is now located in leafy Rathgar, a suburb to the south of Dublin city. However then it was located opposite where Hatch Street now meets Harcourt Street, and was run by two brothers, William and George Wilkins, who were initially kind to Yeats. A classmate, Charles Johnston, he of the Lambay Island adventure, remembers Yeats 'as a lanky youth, with shaggy black hair, markedly good-looking and very talkative … Willie Yeats was strong in mathematics, especially Euclid, and he had a gift for chemistry, but he was no good at all at languages, whether ancient or modern' (*Poet Lore*, 1906).

Another contemporary recorded that Yeats's interest seemed to be entomology, and he constantly carried pill-boxes containing beetles and other insects.

He always carried in his pockets several little cardboard boxes and pill-boxes, filled with his victims, and sometimes the more favoured few were permitted to gaze at their wonderful contents. On one occasion this hobby got him into dire disgrace. One day while in class – history, I think, was the subject – a beetle had the temerity to cross the floor. Nobody made any attempt to interrupt its progress. Suddenly, however, Yeats's eye rested on it. With one bound he was off his seat sprawling on the floor, and soon had his captive in his possession. The master was outraged … and poor

Yeats paid the penalty of having to report himself to the head-master, who severely admonished him.

– T.P.'s Weekly, 1912

Relationships between Willie and his teachers soured towards the end of his time at the High School, chiefly due to his father's own very strict ideas about the shape and substance of a suitable education for his son, and his constant interference in the school's teaching philosophy. So much so that one day the head-master said to young Willie: 'I am going to give you an imposition because I cannot get at your father to give him one' (*Reveries*, 1915).

* * *

John Butler Yeats's studio at 44 York Street swiftly became a focal point for Dublin's bohemian scene, with frequent visits from artists and writers. Late in 1883, JBY moved from York Street to a studio at nearby 7 St. Stephen's Green at forty pounds per year, which he would find difficult to pay. Charles Johnston comments:

Many of the finer qualities of Willie Yeats' mind were formed in the studio on St. Stephen's Green, in long talks on art and life, on man and God, with his sensitive, enthusiastic father. One remembers the long room, with its skylight, the walls of pale green, frames and canvasses massed along them; a sofa and a big armchair or two; the stout iron stove with its tube; and, filling the whole with his spirit, the artist stepping forward along a strip of carpet to touch his work with tentative brush, then stepping back again, always in movement, always meditating high

The poet's father, John Butler Yeats, as a young man

themes, and now and then breaking into talk on the second part of 'Faust,'
or the Hesperian apples, or the relation of villainy to genius.
  – *Poet Lore,* 1906

The new studio saw many now-notable visitors including
Gerard Manley Hopkins, the Jesuit poet, the artists Walter
Osborne and Sarah Purser, as well as sitters including Sir
Hugh Lane, whose art collection would years later become

the topic of much concern and debate for W.B. Yeats, and whose name is now synonymous with the modern-art gallery in Charlemont House on Parnell Square in Dublin.

* * *

In the spring of 1884, the family's financial situation forced them to move from Howth, which they all loved, to a suburb south of Dublin city. There they lived at 10 Ashfield Terrace (now 418 Harold's Cross Road).

We lived in a villa where the red bricks were made pretentious and vulgar with streaks of slate colour, and there seemed to be enemies everywhere.

– Reveries, 1915

The romanticism of Howth had been replaced by a bland suburban landscape; the only compensation, as far as the young Yeats was concerned, was a view of the distant Dublin Mountains. However, JBY saw it as closer to the homes and practices of the professional classes whose portraits he hoped to paint. Unfortunately his anticipated success did not materialise, and the family continued to endure financial hardship to the extent that even the butcher refused to supply them with meat. JBY later wrote that at night, in the interests of economy, they all sat around a single lamp. Willie would …

… begin composing verses, murmuring to himself. He soon forgot the people around him, and his voice grew louder and louder until it filled the

The erstwhile Metropolitan School of Art and the National Library of Ireland, Kildare Street

room. Then his sisters would call out to him, 'Now, Willie, stop compos-
ing!' and he would meekly lower his voice.
  – Prodigal Father, 1978

This chanting would continue until Willie retired to the kitchen, where he could murmur his verses to his heart's content.

* * *

Yeats left the Erasmus Smith High School in December 1883 at the age of eighteen. Though his father had expected him to continue in the family tradition by attending Trinity College, Dublin, Willie's academic aptitude did not meet Trinity's requirements for admission. In May 1884, he enrolled at the Metropolitan School of Art (later the National College of Art and Design), then located in Kildare Street beside the present-day National Library of Ireland. Yeats later complained that he was bored at art school, and that he lacked the temerity to break from his father's style. Nevertheless, art school did introduce him to the poet and mystic George Russell (Æ), who would be a lifelong influence. Yeats said of Russell at this time:

He did not paint the model as we tried to, for some other image rose
always before his eyes (a Saint John in the desert I remember) and already
he spoke to us of his visions. One day he announced he was leaving the
art schools because his will was weak and the arts or any other emotional
pursuit could but weaken it further.
  – Autobiographies, 1927

Russell and Yeats discovered eastern religions together and shared an interest in theosophy and other esoteric beliefs. Both men gradually learned that their talents and enthusiasms lay elsewhere, and despite a dalliance with sculpting, Yeats left art school in April 1886 to concentrate on his writing.

In his early twenties, Yeats's interest in Irish literature, politics and culture was developing feverishly. He met Charles Hubert Oldham, a rising star at Trinity College (later to become a professor there) who organised soirées on Saturday nights at his room on campus to discuss contemporary issues. These meetings were politically charged and the TCD authorities preferred that they take place elsewhere, which forced Oldham to change the venue to a room above Ponsonby's book shop at 116 Grafton Street. This gathering became known as 'the Contemporary Club' and its members – who 'need have nothing in common except that they were all alive at the same moment' – were a diverse bunch that included the academic and future Irish president Douglas Hyde, poet Thomas Rolleston, the recently returned from exile John O'Leary, Land League activist Michael Davitt, James Walker (printer of *The Dublin University Review*, in which Yeats was first published) and many others who were already, or were about to be, part of the cultural and intellectual firmament of Ireland's emerging identity.

Debates would often continue late into the night, and the no-alcohol rule ensured that matters were conducted in a civilised fashion. The 'men only' rule was put aside every fourth Saturday, when women were admitted to a 'symposium'. Among those who attended were Katharine Tynan, artist

Sarah Purser and the poet Ella Young. Maud Gonne also attended but found it dull.

This was also where W.B. Yeats first met textile designer and writer William Morris, whose influence and aesthetic were to rival those of his father. Mary Macken, who also attended the fourth-Saturday events, described W.B.'s speaking style as having 'the stuff of poetry without being that monstrous thing, poetic prose' (Macken, 1939).

In Ireland harsh argument which had gone out of fashion in England was still the manner of our conversation, and at this club Unionist and Nationalist could interrupt one another and insult one another without the formal and traditional restraint of public speech.
– *Reveries,* 1915

Another one to have a profound influence on W.B. Yeats's life was the Fenian John O'Leary, who had been sentenced to twenty years' penal servitude in 1866, the year after Yeats was born. His charge was High Treason (later reduced to Treason Felony) for his membership of the Irish Republican Brotherhood (IRB) and his editorship of the IRB's newspaper, *The Irish People.* He served five years of his sentence in England under very harsh conditions but was released on condition that he remain exiled from Ireland until the full twenty years of his sentence had expired. He spent most of this period in Paris and returned to Ireland in 1885, where he lived at 40 Leinster Road, Rathmines, with his sister Ellen. Yeats first met O'Leary at the Contemporary Club and was immediately drawn to him.

John O'Leary (left) pictured with John MacBride, who would marry Maud Gonne in 1903

He had the moral genius that moves all young people and moves them the more if they are repelled by those who have strict opinions and yet have lived commonplace lives.

– Reveries, 1915

O'Leary hosted many lively gatherings and became a figure of cultural and political authority in the Dublin of the 1880s and 1890s. Yeats recalls his first visit to the O'Leary household:

When I called for the first time at a house in Leinster Road several middle-aged women were playing cards and suggested my taking a hand and gave me a glass of sherry. The sherry went to my head and I was impoverished for days by the loss of sixpence. My hostess was Ellen

O'Leary, who kept house for her brother John O'Leary, the Fenian, the handsomest old man I had ever seen.

– Reveries, 1915

O'Leary, for his part, proclaimed Yeats's poetic genius at every opportunity and took the young poet under his wing. Yeats was later to celebrate O'Leary in his work, perhaps most famously in the poem 'September 1913'.

What need you, being come to sense,
But fumble in a greasy till
And add the halfpence to the pence
And prayer to shivering prayer, until
You have dried the marrow from the bone;
For men were born to pray and save:
Romantic Ireland's dead and gone,
It's with O'Leary in the grave.

Yet they were of a different kind,
The names that stilled your childish play,
They have gone about the world like wind,
But little time had they to pray
For whom the hangman's rope was spun,
And what, God help us, could they save?
Romantic Ireland's dead and gone,
It's with O'Leary in the grave.

Was it for this the wild geese spread
The grey wing upon every tide;
For this that all that blood was shed,

For this Edward Fitzgerald died,
And Robert Emmet and Wolfe Tone,
All that delirium of the brave?
Romantic Ireland's dead and gone,
It's with O'Leary in the grave.

Yet could we turn the years again,
And call those exiles as they were
In all their loneliness and pain,
You'd cry, 'Some woman's yellow hair
Has maddened every mother's son':
They weighed so lightly what they gave.
But let them be, they're dead and gone,
They're with O'Leary in the grave.

– Poems Written in Discouragement, 1913

During 1885 and 1886, W.B. Yeats attended meetings of the Young Ireland Society at 41 York Street, Dublin, close to his father's old studio, which was also the home of the Dublin Workingman's Club. The Young Ireland Society (later the Young Ireland League) was formed in January 1885 to promote Irish nationalism through cultural and literary means, and to encourage original literature by Irish authors. Yeats's impressions of the meetings and his developing sense of his own speech-making and recitative style was recorded in *Reveries*:

A Young Ireland Society met in the lecture-hall of a workmen's club in York Street with O'Leary for president, and there four or five uni-

versity students and myself and occasionally [barrister John Francis] Taylor spoke on Irish history or literature. When Taylor spoke it was a great event, and his delivery in the course of a speech or lecture of some political verse by Thomas Davis gave me a conviction of how great might be the effect of verse, spoken by a man almost rhythm-drunk, at some moment of intensity, the apex of long-mounting thought. Verses that seemed when one saw them upon the page flat and empty caught from that voice, whose beauty was half in its harsh strangeness, nobility and style.

Yeats also records a lively meeting at which 'an excitable man who fought for the Pope against the Italian patriots' (and, who, incidentally, was not one of O'Leary's admirers) opted for violent opposition rather than mere debate when a special meeting was called to move for his expulsion from the Society. Warned that the man was holding his own speech outside in anticipation of attacking those attending the meeting inside, Yeats and others put their backs to the door to prevent the mob from entering.

In a couple of minutes there was a great noise of sticks and broken glass, and after that our landlord came to find out who was to pay for the hall-lamp.
– *Reveries*, 1915

* * *

George Russell (Æ), who shared Yeats's fascination with the occult

Willie Yeats was certainly the centre about which the little literary circle revolved. He was our critic. He brought an extraordinary fresh mind and judgement into our midst.

   – *Reminiscences* by Katharine Tynan, 1913

In June 1885, Katharine Tynan, a poet whose first collection had just been published and a friend of Charles Hubert Oldham (he of the Contemporary Club), received a request from Oldham to meet and discuss her assisting with *The Dublin University Review*, a magazine which Oldham was about to start. Tynan lived with her father, a farmer, at a thatched farmhouse named Whitehall in Clondalkin, about five miles west of Dublin. Throughout the following years, Yeats would visit Whitehall on many occasions both to see Tynan and to attend her literary soirées. Among those who attended these gatherings were Oscar Wilde and his mother Lady Wilde, John and Ellen O'Leary, George Russell (Æ) and Douglas Hyde, as well as John Butler Yeats. Katharine Tynan records her first meeting with the then twenty-year-old Yeats in *Twenty-five Years: Reminiscences* (1913). She was twenty-six at the time. It is widely thought that Yeats proposed to her some years later but she refused him, marrying instead Henry Hinkson in 1893. However, she and Yeats were to remain friends and frequent correspondents for the rest of their lives.

I can remember very well coming into the drawing-room at my old home, which was always filled with a dim green light from the creepers about the windows and the little half-glass door which led into the garden under an arch of boughs – and finding the young men sitting in the bow window … Willie Yeats was at that time of our first meeting twenty years old. He was tall and lanky, and his face was as you would see it in that boyish portrait of him by his father in the Municipal Art Gallery … At that time he was all dreams and all gentleness. The combative tendencies came to him later: such things are apt to develop in Ireland if one is a maker, as they used to call the creative artist long ago. He was beautiful to look at with his dark face, its touch of vivid colouring, the night-black hair, the eager dark eyes. He wore a queer little beard in those days. It was just a little later than his father's portrait of him, and he lived, ate, drank, and slept poetry.

He never minded the five miles' walk through the wintry weather so long as he found at the end a fire, a meal, a bed, and a talk about poetry.

* * *

In *Reveries*, Yeats writes about his fascination with the occult and the paranormal, which began in Sligo while visiting his Middleton and Pollexfen relatives. They shared a strong belief in the other world inhabited by unseen and unaccountable things. In 1885 Yeats and some friends including John Eglinton and Charles Johnston were first exposed to the writings of Alfred Percy Sinnett, including his book *Esoteric Buddhism*, which Yeats received from his enlightened aunt Isabella Pollexfen, who had moved to London. This book introduced these young men, eager for new intellectual experiences, to the doctrines of theosophy. This in turn led to Yeats's exploration of hermeticism, a religious, philosophical and esoteric tradition based on the writings of the Egyptian priest Hermes Trismegistus, with the basic belief that there is a single, fundamental, god-bestowed theology that embraces all religions. Hermeticism also recognised the bond between the emergence of science and its interaction with nature. Yeats later wrote:

I believe in the practice and philosophy of what we have agreed to call magic, in what I must call the evocation of spirits, though I do not know what they are, in the power of creating magical illusion, in the visions of truth in the depths of the mind when the eyes are closed; and I believe in three doctrines, which have, as I think, been handed down from early times and been the foundation of nearly all magical practices. These doctrines are:

(1) That the borders of our minds are ever-shifting, and that many

minds can flow into one another, as it were, and create or reveal a single mind, a single energy.

(2) That the borders of our memories are as shifting, and that our memories are a part of one great memory, the memory of Nature herself.

(3) That this great mind and great memory can be evoked by symbols.

– Ideas of Good and Evil, 1903

In June 1885 Yeats and his friends founded the Dublin Hermetic Society to provide a forum for the discussion of matters of eastern philosophy, the occult, paraphysics and spiritualism. Meetings initially took place at 3 Upper Ely Place, a fine Georgian building near St. Stephen's Green that was also the home of H.M. Magee (John Eglinton's brother) and George Russell (Æ). The society later convened at 13 Eustace Street in Temple Bar.

My friend … and I were reading Baron Reichenbach on Odic Force and manuals published by the Theosophical Society. We spent a good deal of time in the Kildare Street Museum passing our hands over the glass cases, feeling or believing we felt the Odic Force flowing from the big crystals. We also found pins blindfolded and read papers on our discoveries to the Hermetic Society.

– Reveries, 1915

The Dublin Hermetic Society became the Dublin Theosophical Society in April 1886. The Theosophical Society had been founded in New York in 1875 by the Russian Madame Helena Blavatsky and the American Henry Olcott. Madame Blavatsky claimed that its philosophy was related to her via the otherworldly communications of Tibetan mahatmas, whose teachings came to her in the form of secret writings and telepathy. Blavatsky endured accusations of charlatanism, which caused her to leave the United States and end up in London, where a 'lodge' was established in her honour. In April 1886, soon after the founding of the Dublin 'lodge', Mohini Chatterjee was invited to address the Dublin society. Yeats would later write this poem named for the Benghali guru:

'Mohini Chatterjee'

I asked if I should pray,
But the Brahmin said,
'Pray for nothing, say
Every night in bed,
"I have been a king,
I have been a slave,
Nor is there anything.
Fool, rascal, knave,
That I have not been,
And yet upon my breast
A myriad heads have lain."'

That he might set at rest
A boy's turbulent days
Mohini Chatterjee
Spoke these, or words like these.
I add in commentary,
'Old lovers yet may have
All that time denied –
Grave is heaped on grave

That they be satisfied –
Over the blackened earth
The old troops parade,
Birth is heaped on birth
That such cannonade
May thunder time away,
Birth-hour and death-hour meet,
Or, as great sages say,
Men dance on deathless feet.'

– *The Winding Stair*, 1933

* * *

The early 1890s was a period of intense and energetic pursuit of a national literature, and Yeats was at the vanguard. The National Literary Society (NLS) held its inaugural meeting, at which Yeats spoke, on August 16th, 1892, at the Antient Concert Rooms on New Brunswick (now Pearse) Street. Also present were lawyer and poet Charles Gavan Duffy, physician and poet George Sigerson, Fenian John O'Leary, Katharine Tynan, Maud Gonne and Douglas Hyde, who was elected the society's first president. The NLS gave practical support to the idea of an Irish literary revival by distributing Irish-interest books to provincial libraries and the New Irish Library. Another offshoot of the NLS was the Gaelic League, formed in 1893 to promote the Irish language. Its first president was also Douglas Hyde.

The Antient Concert Rooms also hosted the inaugural production of the Irish Literary Theatre (ILT), founded by Yeats,

Lady Augusta Gregory and Edward Martyn; Yeats's play *The Countess Cathleen* was staged on May 8th, 1899, with Florence Farr in the leading role. Two days prior to the first performance, Yeats wrote an article in *Literature* in which he stated:

> *Our plays will all be about Irish subjects; and, if we can find enough writers, and I have little doubt we will find them, who will write with some depth and simplicity about Irish legends associated with the rivers and mountains of Ireland, or about Irish personages and events, or about modern Irish life, an increasing number of persons will desire to hear a message that will so often illustrate the circumstance of their lives.*
> – *Collected Works IX*, 2010

The Countess Cathleen was not without controversy, with its Faustian theme in which the main character sells her soul to feed starving peasants yet still rises to heaven. This incited the anger of the Catholic hierarchy, and protests threatened to disrupt the opening night. In anticipation of trouble, Yeats requested that there be a police presence; however, despite a certain amount of hissing, the evening passed off without incident. One member of the audience that night was James Joyce, who recorded the evening in his novel *A Portrait of the Artist as a Young Man*.

For its second and third seasons, the ILT moved to the Gaiety Theatre on South King Street near St. Stephen's Green. There they performed Edward Martyn's *Maeve*, Alice Milligan's *The Last Feast of the Fianna* and George Moore's *The Bending of the Bough* in 1890, and Douglas Hyde's *Casadh an tSúgáin (The Twisting of the Rope)* and *Diarmuid and Grainne* by Yeats and George Moore (an unhappy collaboration!) in 1891. The plays – except for Hyde's, which was performed in Irish by members of the Gaelic League, with the author in the lead role – were performed in English by British actors using British sets.

In 1901 the Irish Literary Theatre disbanded and the Irish National Theatre Society was formed with the express intention of using Irish actors in Irish plays by Irish playwrights. Yeats himself was president, and the vice-presidents were Maud Gonne, Douglas Hyde and George Russell (Æ). Frank and William Fay, two brothers who acted and directed, joined the society and brought with them a pioneering enthusiasm and a desire to see the establishment of an Irish theatrical tradition.

John Millington Synge

IRISH NATIONAL THEATRE SOCIETY

SPREADING THE NEWS
By LADY GREGORY.

ON BAILE'S STRAND
and

KATHLEEN NI HOULIHAN
By W. B. YEATS.

IN THE SHADOW OF THE GLEN
By J. M. SYNGE.

ABBEY THEATRE
TUESDAY, DEC. 27, '04
TO
TUESDAY, JAN. 3, '05.

Stalls, 3s. Reserved and Numbered. Balcony, 2s. Reserved and Numbered. Pit, 1s

Seats can be booked at Cramer, Wood & Co's, Westmoreland St.

Printed by An Cló-Cumann, Limited, Gaelic Printers, Great Strand Street, Dublin.

The society first used St. Teresa's Hall in Clarendon Street, where the Fay brothers' productions included Yeats's *Cathleen Ni Houlihan* in 1902, with Maud Gonne in the title role. Then they moved to 34 Camden Street and Molesworth Hall for performances of *The Hour Glass* and *The King's Threshold* by Yeats, *Twenty-Five* by Lady Gregory, *Broken Soil* by Padraic Colum, and perhaps most notably *In the Shadow of the Glen* by J.M. Synge, which caused public protests when it was first performed in October 1903 due to its heroine's perceived immorality in leaving home to take up with a wanderer.

It soon became clear that the Irish National Theatre Society required its own permanent home. In 1904, Annie Horniman, heiress to the Horniman tea fortune, took out a lease on the Mechanic Institute on Abbey Street and the neighbouring morgue on Marlborough Street for 170 pounds per annum. Using the architect Joseph Holloway, the buildings were joined and renovated to provide a large stage and dressing rooms, as well as seating for upwards of 550 people. The result was the Abbey Theatre, created using Irish craftsmanship wherever possible including the portraits of the leading figures by John Butler Yeats and the stained glass by Sarah Purser. Between 1905 and 1907, additional properties were purchased.

On December 27th, 1904, the Abbey Theatre finally opened to a packed house with performances of Yeats's *On Baile's Strand* and *Cathleen Ni Houlihan* as well as Lady Gregory's *Spreading the News*. Annie Horniman subsidised the theatre until 1910 when, due to a deteriorating relationship with Lady Gregory and Yeats that reached its culmination when the Abbey failed to close its doors for the death of King Edward VII in May

1910, she sold the lease and the title to the Irish National Theatre Society for one thousand pounds.

Some of Yeats's finest moments were to come in defence of plays staged at the Abbey. In January 1907, at the first performance of J.M. Synge's *The Playboy of the Western World*, there was public outcry and rioting at the play's depiction of Irish mores and the use of the word 'shift' on stage. According to a report by Mary Colum, Yeats 'took the stage in full evening dress and step by step he interpreted the play saying "the author of *Cathleen Ni Houlihan* addresses you".' She added: 'I have never witnessed a human being fight as Yeats fought that night, nor knew another with so many weapons in his armory' ('Memories of Yeats', 1939).

On the stage with him was his father, John Butler Yeats. Yeats talks about this moment in his poem 'Beautiful Lofty Things':

Beautiful lofty things; O'Leary's noble head;
My father upon the Abbey stage, before him a raging crowd.
'This Land of Saints,' and then as the applause died out,
'Of plaster Saints'; his beautiful mischievous head thrown back.
Standish O'Grady supporting himself between the tables
Speaking to a drunken audience high nonsensical words;
Augusta Gregory seated at her great ormolu table,
Her eightieth winter approaching; 'Yesterday he threatened my life,
I told him that nightly from six to seven I sat at this table
The blinds drawn up'; Maud Gonne at Howth station waiting a train,
Pallas Athena in that straight back and arrogant head:
All the Olympians; a thing never known again.

– New Poems, 1938

Yeats's fearlessness and his conviction that Ireland had to see herself in an honest light continued throughout his life and was revealed again in his defence of Sean O'Casey's *The Plough and the Stars* two decades later, in February 1926. This time Irish nationalists felt that the play belittled and slandered those who had died during the Easter Rising of 1916. On the fourth night of the play, a crowd comprising mainly women related to the fallen heroes stormed the stage and the riots commenced. Yeats responded with his now famous words:

You have disgraced yourselves again. Is this to be an ever-recurring celebration of the arrival of Irish genius? Once more you have rocked the cradle of genius. The news of what is happening here will go from country to country. You have once more rocked the cradle of reputation. The fame of O'Casey is born tonight.

In August 1925 the government finally offered the financially flailing Abbey Theatre a lifeline in the form of a guaranteed subsidy, which was 850 pounds in the first year. Yeats and his friend and supporter Lady Gregory had first started to shape the dream of a national theatre on a wet afternoon in June 1896 in Duras House, Galway (an event which will be examined in more detail later), and from its humble and inauspicious beginnings, it was now a reality. The Peacock, an experimental theatre and teaching space, opened in November 1926.

In 1951 a fire destroyed much of the stage and dressing room areas of the original building. The Abbey relocated to the Queen's Theatre on Pearse Street until, fifteen years later, it reopened on Abbey Street with an increased capacity of over six hundred people.

John Singer Sargent, 'Portrait of
Sir Hugh Lane', 1906

* * *

In the first decade of the twentieth century, Yeats was in the thick of things social, cultural and political, and once he identified something worth fighting for, he fought. He was invested in literary movements and the effort to breathe life into a national theatre; in a similar vein, and perhaps at greater risk to his own growing reputation as an esteemed man of letters, he went into battle for the visual arts.

Cork-born Hugh Lane, Lady Gregory's nephew, was an art dealer and collector specialising in modern European art. He had amassed a collection, known as 'the French Paintings', of thirty-nine works by the leading artists of the period including Manet, Monet, Renoir, Degas and Vuillard. Lane promised the collection to the city of Dublin on the condition that the city provide a suitable building in which to house it. Lane was also a great promoter of Irish art abroad and considered it essential that Ireland have its own gallery of modern art exhibiting the works of modern Irish artists. However, the city council's unanimous support was not forthcoming. The debate raged over whether art could be considered necessary for the public good, or if an impoverished Dublin could afford to support what some saw as an expensive luxury when there were more pressing social problems that the money could help address.

Hugh Lane founded the Dublin Municipal Gallery in Clonmell House at 17 Harcourt Street in 1907. The city council promised some financial support for this enterprise, but for various legal reasons it was unable, or unwilling, to fulfill its promise until 1911. Meanwhile Lane supported the gallery himself. The campaign to find a suitable building intensified, with Yeats and Lady Gregory playing prominent and public roles. Nevertheless, though the city would not fully support the provision of a gallery for the French Paintings, it did pledge twenty-two thousand pounds to the project, and Yeats, Gregory and others began a campaign to raise the rest. The Abbey Theatre pledged one thousand pounds, which caused unrest among the actors as they were sacrificing some of their earnings for a cause they didn't necessarily support. The Abbey's tour of America in 1913 was seen as part-fundraiser for the gallery, and the administration sold souvenir handkerchiefs embossed with lines from a Yeats poem written in support of the gallery to raise money.

In December 1912 Yeats, in his frustration at the reticence of the public to support the campaign, wrote the berating poem 'To a Wealthy Man Who Promised a Second Subscription to the Dublin Municipal Gallery if It Were Proved the People Wanted Pictures', which was first published in *The Irish Times*.

> *You gave, but will not give again*
> *Until enough of Paudeen's pence*
> *By Biddy's halfpennies have lain*
> *To be 'some sort of evidence',*
> *Before you'll put your guineas down,*
> *That things it were a pride to give*
> *Are what the blind and ignorant town*
> *Imagines best to make it thrive.*
> *What cared Duke Ercole, that bid*

His mummers to the market-place,
What th' onion-sellers thought or did
So that his Plautus set the pace
For the Italian comedies?
And Guidobaldo, when he made
That grammar school of courtesies
Where wit and beauty learned their trade
Upon Urbino's windy hill,
Had sent no runners to and fro
That he might learn the shepherds' will.
And when they drove out Cosimo,
Indifferent how the rancour ran,
He gave the hours they had set free
To Michelozzo's latest plan
For the San Marco Library,
Whence turbulent Italy should draw
Delight in Art whose end is peace,
In logic and in natural law
By sucking at the dugs of Greece.
Your open hand but shows our loss,
For he knew better how to live.
Let Paudeens play at pitch and toss,
Look up in the sun's eye and give
What the exultant heart calls good
That some new day may breed the best
Because you gave, not what they would,
But the right twigs for an eagle's nest!

– Poems Written in Discouragement, 1913

By 1913, against a background of labour strikes and general political unrest in Ireland, a gallery design by the English architect Edwin Lutyens was presented to the city council. It proposed an enclosed bridge-gallery that would span the River Liffey at the place where the Ha'penny Bridge stands today. The ambitious plan garnered support but not enough to achieve approval. The cost was estimated at forty-five thousand pounds, which was a substantial amount of money in 1913. The Lutyens design attracted the support of Hugh Lane and Yeats, among others. When it was rejected by Dublin City Council in September 1913, Yeats was incensed. His series *Poems Written in Discouragement*, which included 'September 1913', below, left the public in no doubt as to Yeats's feelings about the response to an appeal for financial support for something he saw as integral to the cultural life of a nation in renaissance.

> *What need you, being come to sense,*
> *But fumble in a greasy till*
> *And add the halfpence to the pence*
> *And prayer to shivering prayer, until*
> *You have dried the marrow from the bone;*
> *For men were born to pray and save:*
> *Romantic Ireland's dead and gone,*
> *It's with O'Leary in the grave.*

In October 1913, and in reaction to the rejection of the Lutyens design, Lane bequeathed the French Paintings to the National Gallery in London instead, which promised him the suitable exhibition space he craved. However, a disagreement with the National Gallery in 1915 prompted him to write a codicil to his will bequeathing the paintings back to Dublin. Though the codicil was signed, it was not witnessed – a fact that had long-lasting consequences after Lane died in 1915 aboard the *Lusitania*, which was torpedoed by a German submarine off the coast of Cork. The National Gallery in London held on to the paintings, claiming that the codicil was not legally binding. This set in motion decades of disputed ownership, which was finally resolved by sharing the collection between Ireland and England, exchanging parts every five years. Yeats, in a Senate speech on May 9th, 1923, agitated for the return of the paintings:

In fighting to recover these pictures you [the Senate] are fighting for a unique possession which will always remain unique and always give prestige to the Gallery that contains it.
– *The Senate Speeches*, 1960

Finally, in 1933, the Municipal Gallery of Modern Art opened in Charlemont House on Parnell Square North; it is now known as Dublin City Gallery: The Hugh Lane. Though it did not happen in his lifetime, the realisation of Lane's ambition was fought for in verse, coin and debate by Yeats.

Late in life, in a poem of reminiscence, Yeats celebrated this national achievement in 'The Municipal Gallery Revisited', written in 1937:

I

Around me the images of thirty years:
An ambush; pilgrims at the water-side;
Casement upon trial, half hidden by the bars,
Guarded; Griffith staring in hysterical pride;
Kevin O'Higgins' countenance that wears
A gentle questioning look that cannot hide
A soul incapable of remorse or rest;
A revolutionary soldier kneeling to be blessed.

II

An Abbot or Archbishop with an upraised hand
Blessing the Tricolour. 'This is not,' I say,
'The dead Ireland of my youth, but an Ireland
The poets have imagined, terrible and gay.'
Before a woman's portrait suddenly I stand;
Beautiful and gentle in her Venetian way.
I met her all but fifty years ago
For twenty minutes in some studio.

III

Heart-smitten with emotion I sink down,
My heart recovering with covered eyes;
Wherever I had looked I had looked upon
My permanent or impermanent images;
Augusta Gregory's son; her sister's son,
Hugh Lane, 'onlie begetter' of all these;
Hazel Lavery living and dying, that tale
As though some ballad-singer had sung it all.

IV

Mancini's portrait of Augusta Gregory,
'Greatest since Rembrandt,' according to John Synge;

A great ebullient portrait certainly;
But where is the brush that could show anything
Of all that pride and that humility?
And I am in despair that time may bring
Approved patterns of women or of men
But not that selfsame excellence again.

V

My mediaeval knees lack health until they bend,
But in that woman, in that household where
Honour had lived so long, all lacking found.
Childless I thought, 'My children may find here
Deep-rooted things,' but never foresaw its end,

Dublin City Gallery: The Hugh Lane

And now that end has come I have not wept;
No fox can foul the lair the badger swept.

VI

(An image out of Spenser and the common tongue.)
John Synge, I and Augusta Gregory, thought
All that we did, all that we said or sang
Must come from contact with the soil, from that
Contact everything Antaeus-like grew strong.
We three alone in modern times had brought
Everything down to that sole test again,
Dream of the noble and the beggarman.

VII

And here's John Synge himself, that rooted man
'Forgetting human words,' a grave deep face.
You that would judge me, do not judge alone
This book or that, come to this hallowed place
Where my friends' portraits hang and look thereon;
Ireland's history in their lineaments trace;
Think where man's glory most begins and ends
And say my glory was I had such friends.

– New Poems, 1938

* * *

His father's studio was not to be Yeats's only connection with St. Stephen's Green in the early 1880s. Laura Armstrong, whom we already met on the slopes of the Hill of Howth, also lived there at 60 St. Stephen's Green, and the love-smitten Yeats tells of trying to visit her to discuss *The Island of Statues*, the

'I was twenty-three years old when the troubling of my life began': W.B. Yeats on his first meeting with Maud Gonne. Photographed here by Jean Reutlinger

play he had written for her. On August 10th, 1884, Yeats called to her house, as arranged, but she was not home. He penned a note to her indicating his disappointment. Laura referred to herself as 'Vivien' (hence the play of that name that Yeats wrote for her) and he was 'Clarin'. 'Vivien' soon responded, writing,

My dear Clarin … I hope you will forgive me. It so happened that I was positively obliged to go out at the hour I had appointed for you to come but it was only to a house quite close to here … I looked out of the window and to my great disappointment saw my Clarin leaving No. 60 … I like your poems more than I can say – but I should like to hear you read them … I shall be in all Tuesday afternoon. I promise! So can you come? … Trusting to see 'the poet' – Believe me Ever yours 'Vivien'
– Letters, 1954

Within a month the same 'Vivien' had married Henry Byrne and crushed all hopes the young Yeats might have had of wooing her himself.

Just around the corner, 73 St. Stephen's Green belonged to Maud Gonne, who was imprisoned in May 1918 in Holloway Prison for her role in campaigning against conscription to the British Army. While incarcerated Gonne sublet the house to Yeats and his wife George for four months at fifty shillings a week. In October 1918 Yeats, in a blaze of domesticity, wrote to George, who was pregnant and in England, to describe his progress with furnishing the house. He wrote:

We bought yesterday for $7.11.0 one chest of drawers (not bad) two small tables (one mahogany and quite decent) two wash stands … The

furniture when we are done with it can be sold at an auction room &
should fetch a very good price.

 – *W.B. Yeats and George Yeats: The Letters,* 2011

But the scene of domestic bliss was swiftly shattered. Imprisoned Gonne was in poor health and, in addition, she had received news that her sister Kathleen and Lucien Millevoye, her lover and the father of her daughter Iseult, had both died. Thanks in part to Yeats's interventions Gonne was released on compassionate grounds in November 1918 and, in disguise as a nurse – under the terms of her release, she was forbidden to travel to Ireland – she made straight for Dublin and 73 St. Stephen's Green. Yeats refused to admit her, suspecting that Gonne's presence might cause a level of drama that his pregnant wife, suffering from influenza, would find troubling. He also quite reasonably feared raids by the authorities searching for the fugitive Gonne. Nevertheless Yeats recognised that he could not stay on at the house and took rooms at 96 St. Stephen's Green during the winter of 1918–1919, leaving it on February 22nd, four days before his daughter Anne was born at a Dublin nursing home.

The confrontation with Gonne led to a rift that took some years, and another dramatic Gonne experience, to mend. This time it would be Iseult's turn to be central to the drama. Having twice refused Yeats's proposal of marriage, in 1916 and 1917 (Yeats was fifty-one and fifty-two when he proposed to Iseult, who was in her early twenties; he would go on to marry the twenty-five-year-old Georgie 'George' Hyde-Lees in October 1917), Iseult had married the young poet and novelist Francis

Iseult Gonne

Stuart, and they lived in a house bought by Maud at Baravore, Glenmalure, Co. Wicklow.

The marriage was not going well and, in July 1920, almost two years after their confrontation on the doorstep of 73 St. Stephen's Green, Maud Gonne asked Yeats to intervene and mediate in her daughter's marriage breakdown. He went to stay with Iseult and Stuart and found the young woman unwell and exhausted, claiming that her husband had denied her food and sleep. Yeats arranged for Iseult to be treated in Dublin and brokered a separation from Stuart, which did not last. It transpired that Iseult was also pregnant; the baby was born in March 1921 but died four months later. Despite Yeats's interventions Iseult and Stuart reconciled and maintained a difficult relationship until 1939, when Stuart left for Berlin.

Iseult features in a number of Yeats's poems including 'Why Should Not Old Men Be Mad?' from *On the Boiler* (1938), in which he comments on his love for her, the 'girl who knew all Dante once', and the disparity in age as well as her 'dunce' husband Stuart:

Why should not old men be mad?
Some have known a likely lad
That had a sound fly-fisher's wrist
Turn to a drunken journalist;
A girl that knew all Dante once
Live to bear children to a dunce;
A Helen of social welfare dream,
Climb on a wagonette to scream.
Some think it a matter of course that chance
Should starve good men and bad advance,
That if their neighbours figured plain,
As though upon a lighted screen,
No single story would they find
Of an unbroken happy mind,
A finish worthy of the start.
Young men know nothing of this sort,
Observant old men know it well;
And when they know what old books tell
And that no better can be had,
Know why an old man should be mad.

* * *

In his later life, Yeats frequently travelled between London, Dublin, Galway and Sligo. He was a familiar guest at a number of Dublin hotels where he would take rooms. Indeed, many of his friends and associates did the same, meeting, dining and sleeping beneath the one roof. By 1914 Yeats had become a member of the Stephen's Green Club at 9 St. Stephen's Green. He was there during the war years and the tumultuous period of Irish history that climaxed with the Easter Rising of 1916. At the end of March of that year, and less than a month before the Rising took place in Dublin, he wrote to his friend Arthur Symons:

I stay now at this Club, an old building, 18th Century, with fine cealings [sic] *& looking out on the ornamental garden of Stephen's Green.*
– *Letters*, 1954

Yeats craved conversation but found only bridge and empty gossip at the club. He left it in 1922 to become a member of the University Club by virtue of the honorary doctorate that Trinity College bestowed on him, and lastly the Kildare Street Club (now amalgamated with the University Club at 17 St. Stephen's Green). Finally, to his satisfaction, he found more conversation and less bridge.

Yeats does not ignore the 'club-scene' in his poetry – that bastion of the Victorian establishment and the upper middle classes. In one of his best-known poems, 'Easter 1916', he refers to the cosy comfort of those members sitting around a fire who appeared removed from the violent commotion that was taking place 'among grey eighteenth-century houses' on the streets outside.

I have met them at close of day
Coming with vivid faces
From counter or desk among grey
Eighteenth-century houses.
I have passed with a nod of the head
Or polite meaningless words,
Or have lingered awhile and said
Polite meaningless words,
And thought before I had done
Of a mocking tale or a gibe
To please a companion
Around the fire at the club,
Being certain that they and I
But lived where motley is worn:
All changed, changed utterly:
A terrible beauty is born.

– Michael Robartes and the Dancer, 1921

Where Yeats once looked out onto the ornamental garden in Stephen's Green can now be found the Yeats Memorial Garden, slightly removed from the bustle of the main pathways that criss-cross the park. Here in a quiet almost auditorium is an abstract bronze statue of Yeats sculpted by Henry Moore in 1967, depicting the poet with cape and arms flailing, embodying all the swirling energy and majesty of his life and work.

* * *

The early 1920s were exciting years of public engagement and acclaim for Yeats. Living through the Irish War of Independence and its unsteady truce in July 1921, and then a period of intense negotiation between the British and Irish that resulted in the Anglo-Irish Treaty in December of that year, Yeats found himself increasingly drawn into the troubled waters that surrounded him. When the Treaty was rejected by Éamon de Valera and others and the Civil War ensued, Yeats came out on the Pro-Treaty side of the argument. The Civil War lasted from June 1922 until May 1923, and Ireland would never be the same again. As Yeats wrote:

> *Now and in time to be,*
> *Wherever green is worn,*
> *Are changed, changed utterly:*
> *A terrible beauty is born.*

> *– Michael Robartes and the Dancer,* 1921

Yeats's stature as an influential public figure was formally recognised in December 1922 when he was appointed to the first Senate by William T. Cosgrave, who became the president of the Executive Council of the Irish Free State in the wake of the Civil War.

Just before Yeats's elevation to the political establishment, he and George purchased a grand Georgian house at 82 Merrion Square, one of Dublin's most elegant addresses. Its large rooms and high ceilings gave the Yeatses a sense of opulent comfort they had not known before, even though its purchase and decoration created a considerable financial strain. This was exacerbated around that time by the financial difficulties of the Cuala Industries, a business run by Yeats's sisters, Lily (Susan Mary) and Lolly (Elizabeth Corbet), for which he felt somewhat responsible.

But Yeats's Senate appointment also provided him with a steady income of 360 pounds per annum; not a huge sum, perhaps, but suddenly, and for the first time in his life, he had some degree of financial security.

Yeats's appointment by Cosgrave to the Senate – partly in recognition of his contributions to the cultural dynamic that was emerging in Ireland, but also rumoured to be due to his earlier membership of the secretive Irish Republican Brotherhood – was seen to be little political threat to either

George and W.B. Yeats

The 1924 Tailteann Games Committee, of which W.B. Yeats (fourth from right at the back) was chairman, outside the headquarters of the RIA at 19 Dawson Street. Also among the group are Eoin O'Duffy, Kevin O'Higgins, William T. Cosgrave, Desmond FitzGerald and Chief Justice Kennedy.

side. Nonetheless his home, like those of the other senators, became a 'legitimate' target for the Anti-Treaty faction. In October 1922 a bomb exploded in Merrion Square, shattering the windows of the Yeatses' house. Even more ominous was the firing of two bullets through the windows on Christmas Eve of the same year, which sent plaster raining down from the nursery ceiling where George was sitting with baby Anne. George was hit by bullet fragments. A sentry had been posted to the corner of Merrion Square after the first attack, but that clearly failed to prevent the second. Yeats spent a good deal of this period in England, staying for the most part in the Savile Club at 107 Piccadilly, but he was greatly concerned about George's safety and exhorted her to join him in England. However George was insistent on staying and felt strongly that the conflict was drawing to a close – which it did in May 1923.

As a senator, Yeats served on a number of influential committees, chiefly the Irish Manuscript Committee, which concerned itself with the preservation and promotion of the Irish language. His chairmanship of the Coinage Committee – and his widely acknowledged authorship of its report, written in language that is still upheld as a model of lucidity and precision – resulted in the minting of coins that bore images of Irish animals, birds and the Irish harp. Yeats was very vocal on issues such as divorce, arguing for the separation of Church and State, and the rights of the Protestant minority in the Republic of Ireland. He was also outspoken on the subject of censorship, which he abhorred.

It is not surprising, given the unorthodox nature of his own education, that he should have strong opinions on this matter also. He believed in the democracy of education, insisting that it should be for all people regardless of economic or social background. In March 1926 Yeats's passion for education took him in his capacity as senator to St. Otteran's Montessori School in Waterford, which was seen as a progressive educational departure for its time. Yeats, now 'a sixty-year-old smiling public man' was impressed by the pupils and visited the school on two consecutive days. The visit inspired his 1927 poem 'Among School Children', which evokes a vast range of imagery including clear references to Maud Gonne, envisioning her standing there as a child, possessing something of the common world that she, in his mind, managed to escape.

I

I walk through the long schoolroom questioning;
A kind old nun in a white hood replies;
The children learn to cipher and to sing,
To study reading-books and history,
To cut and sew, be neat in everything
In the best modern way – the children's eyes
In momentary wonder stare upon
A sixty-year-old smiling public man.

II

I dream of a Ledaean body, bent
Above a sinking fire, a tale that she
Told of a harsh reproof, or trivial event
That changed some childish day to tragedy –
Told, and it seemed that our two natures blent
Into a sphere from youthful sympathy,
Or else, to alter Plato's parable,
Into the yolk and white of the one shell.

III

And thinking of that fit of grief or rage
I look upon one child or t'other there
And wonder if she stood so at that age –
For even daughters of the swan can share
Something of every paddler's heritage –
And had that colour upon cheek or hair,

Jack and W.B. pictured outside their sisters'
home, Gurteen Dhas ('pretty little field'), on
Lower Churchtown Road.

And thereupon my heart is driven wild:
She stands before me as a living child.

IV

Her present image floats into the mind –
Did Quattrocento finger fashion it
Hollow of cheek as though it drank the wind
And took a mess of shadows for its meat?
And I though never of Ledaean kind
Had pretty plumage once – enough of that,
Better to smile on all that smile, and show
There is a comfortable kind of old scarecrow.

V

What youthful mother, a shape upon her lap
Honey of generation had betrayed,
And that must sleep, shriek, struggle to escape
As recollection or the drug decide,
Would think her son, did she but see that shape
With sixty or more winters on its head,
A compensation for the pang of his birth,
Or the uncertainty of his setting forth?

VI

Plato thought nature but a spume that plays
Upon a ghostly paradigm of things;
Solider Aristotle played the taws
Upon the bottom of a king of kings;
World-famous golden-thighed Pythagoras
Fingered upon a fiddle-stick or strings
What a star sang and careless Muses heard:
Old clothes upon old sticks to scare a bird.

VII

Both nuns and mothers worship images,
But those the candles light are not as those
That animate a mother's reveries,
But keep a marble or a bronze repose.
And yet they too break hearts – O Presences
That passion, piety or affection knows,
And that all heavenly glory symbolise –
O self-born mockers of man's enterprise;

VIII

Labour is blossoming or dancing where
The body is not bruised to pleasure soul,
Nor beauty born out of its own despair,
Nor blear-eyed wisdom out of midnight oil.
O chestnut tree, great rooted blossomer,
Are you the leaf, the blossom or the bole?
O body swayed to music, O brightening glance,
How can we know the dancer from the dance?

– The Tower, 1928

In contrast to the Ledaean beauty to which Yeats refers in the poem, a thirteen-year-old student who attended St. Otteran's at the time wrote later that he 'watched from a window as Senator W.B. Yeats, in soft hat and with magisterial presence, took his distinguished way up the driveway of St. Otteran's School. His famed turkey strut – a gait combining short, jerky steps with body erect, head thrown back and hands clasped behind his back – was unforgettable' (Donald T. Torchiana, 1965).

W.B. and George's home at 82 Merrion Square

In June 1925 Yeats had a particularly busy period in the Senate, making speeches about the need for Ireland to preserve its national monuments and statues. He also spoke passionately against the prohibition of divorce, a topic that affected him deeply as he felt it discriminated against the Protestant minority. He railed against the piety of the Catholic majority following the Church's claims that Ireland was built upon a foundation of purity. In 'The Three Monuments', written in 1927, he succinctly directs his anger at this perceived hypocrisy, mentioning the three statues on O'Connell Street in Dublin beneath which the politicians and their supporters rallied: those of O'Connell, Parnell and Nelson, whose pillar still stood in the middle of the street. All three 'old rascals' were Protestants, and two of them are national heroes.

They hold their public meetings where
Our most renowned patriots stand,
One among the birds of the air,
A stumpier on either hand;
And all the popular statesmen say
That purity built up the State
And after kept it from decay;
And let all base ambition be,
For intellect would make us proud
And pride bring in impurity:
The three old rascals laugh aloud.

– The Tower, 1928

One of Yeats's concerns as a resident of Merrion Square, a private, key-holder park at the time, was the under-utilisation of its resources. In 1927 there was a movement among some residents to open it up to the general public and to children in particular as a playground. In a speech to the Senate on March 9th, Yeats generously stated:

> *Very occasionally, perhaps once a year, I go and walk in that Square. We use it very little, and I notice that there are generally children there who have no legal right to be there. The railing is in bad repair and they go in. I should like those children to have a legal right to play in that Square. I should like the Square to be made available for them. Almost every day I go round the waters in Stephen's Green. I know the great delight that that Square and these waters give children.*
> – *The Senate Speeches*, 1960

Despite Yeats's impassioned plea, the park was not opened to the public until the 1960s.

Though Yeats undoubtedly derived a great deal from and contributed in important ways to the Senate, he advised his friend Ezra Pound against being elected, disillusioned as he was by his unsuitability for public office when there were those 'old lawyers, old bankers, old business men, who because all habit and memory, have begun to govern the world. They lean over the chair in front and talk as if to half a dozen of their kind at some board-meeting, and, whether they carry their point or not, retain moral ascendancy' (*A Vision*, 1925).

On November 15th, 1923, Yeats was awarded the Nobel Prize for Literature. With this great recognition came 7,500 pounds, with which he continued to furnish 82 Merrion Square and pay off his sister Lily's medical expenses and the debts incurred by Cuala Industries.

In order to place Cuala Industries on an even sounder footing, the business moved into the basement of the Merrion Square house in August 1923, with Yeats's wife George assuming the role of supervisor of the embroidery section in the absence of the ill Lily. George maintained an active role in the company for the rest of her life.

In anticipation of the termination of his Senate appointment, the Yeatses sold 82 Merrion Square in May 1928 for fifteen hundred pounds. Yeats's health was deteriorating, and he was advised that the damp Irish winters were becoming increasingly harmful. In March 1928 they signed a five-year lease on an apartment in Rapallo, Italy, where Yeats had visited his friend Ezra Pound on numerous occasions during the 1920s and 1930s. This was to be a frequent destination for the Yeatses over the coming years, interspersed with visits to Switzerland, France and Spain. However, they were still persuaded

The Dublin Mountains near Riversdale, Rathfarnham, with the Hellfire Club in the distance

that they needed a Dublin address, so they moved one Georgian square over to 42 Fitzwilliam Square, where Jack also had a studio at number 18. They remained there until July 1932, with a brief three-month interlude in early 1931 in a house on South Hill, Killiney, owned by the publisher and, later, biographer of Yeats, Joseph Hone.

* * *

When the Yeats family left 42 Fitzwilliam Square, they took a thirteen-year lease on Riversdale, a rambling eighteenth-century farmhouse at Willbrook, Rathfarnham, off the Ballyboden Road. The poet, now sixty-seven years old and ailing, found that Riversdale possessed all the attractions of country life, with its gardens, its peace and quiet, while also being close to Dublin, just four or five miles distant from the city centre. George decorated the house in preparation for the move, and Yeats was excited by the prospect of enjoying the gardens. He wrote a number of letters to his erstwhile lover Olivia Shakespear in late June and early July of 1932 describing the house and its gardens:

I hope I shall there re-create in some measure the routine that was my life at Coole, the only place where I have ever had unbroken health. I am just too far from Dublin to go there without good reason and too far, I hope, for most interviewers and the less determined travelling bores. I shall have a big old fruit garden all to myself – the study opens into it and it is shut off from the flower garden and the croquet and tennis lawns and from the bowling green. George is painting my walls lemon

'Being high and solitary and most stern': Maud Gonne

yellow and the doors green and black. We have a lease for thirteen years
but that will see me out.
  – *Letters,* 1954

Later that year, in another letter to Shakespear, Yeats proudly
gives a more detailed description of the house and flowers,
discussing a picture of himself and the house that appeared in
the *Dublin Evening Mail.*

The downstairs right-window is that of my study (there is a glass door behind the conservatory from study to garden and a window into the conservatory). It is a long room, walls and ceiling all lemon yellow. It is full of pictures. The room upstairs is my bedroom and there too is another window (not shown) where the meat bone hangs for the tomtits. The great flowers in the portrait of myself are poker flowers. We are surrounded by trees.

– Letters, 1954

Yeats enjoyed the company of women throughout his life; his own accounts, his letters and evidence provided by numerous biographers suggest intimate encounters both before and after his marriage to George. These include his relationships with Florence Farr, Dorothy Wellesley and Maud Gonne – the last was eventually consummated in December 1908 in Paris – and his pursuit of Gonne's daughter Iseult, to whom

he proposed during the summers of 1916 of 1917.

The poet's final mistress, for the last two years of his life, was the renowned journalist Edith Shackleton Heald. She lived at the Chantry House in Steyning, Surrey, and Yeats became a frequent visitor there between 1937 and 1939. Shackleton Heald went to France with Yeats and George in 1938, and both women were at his bedside when he died at the Hôtel Idéal Séjour in Roquebrune-Cap-Martin in January 1939. It was in a letter to Shackleton Heald written in late November 1937, as his health was deteriorating and he became increasingly convinced that he might never be able to show his friends his home in person, that Yeats gave the most intimate description of his study at Riversdale.

All round the study walls are book-cases but some stop half way up and over them are pictures by my brother, my father, by Robert Gregory. On each of the windows into the flower garden are two great Chinese pictures (Dulac's gift) and in the window into the greenhouse hangs a most lovely Burne-Jones window (Ricketts's gift). Through the glass door into the flower garden I see the bare boughs of apple trees and a few last flowers.
– Letters, 1954

It was in August 1938 at Riversdale that Yeats and Maud Gonne met for the final time. Gonne noticed how ill and weak Yeats had become. Their conversation turned to a dream they had in the early days of their friendship, to find a 'Castle of the Heroes' in the middle of a lake, 'a shrine of Irish tradition where only those who had dedicated their lives to Ireland might penetrate':

Our Castle of the Heroes remained a Castle in the Air, but the last time I saw Willie at Riversdale just before he left Ireland for the last time, as we said goodbye, he, sitting in his arm-chair from which he could rise only with great effort, said, 'Maud, we should have gone on with our Castle of the Heroes, we might still do it'. I was so surprised that he remembered, I could not reply.

– Scattering Branches, 1940

On October 25th, 1938, Yeats left Riversdale for the last time, crossing to London before eventually travelling to the South of France where he died three months later. After his death, George found the house and gardens too costly to maintain and relinquished the lease, moving to 46 Palmerston Road in Rathmines, where she brought up their two children, Anne and Michael, and continued to manage the affairs of Cuala Industries until her death in 1968.

'An Acre of Grass'

Picture and book remain,
An acre of green grass
For air and exercise,
Now strength of body goes;
Midnight, an old house
Where nothing stirs but a mouse.

My temptation is quiet.
Here at life's end
Neither loose imagination,
Nor the mill of the mind
Consuming its rag and bone,
Can make the truth known.

Grant me an old man's frenzy,
Myself must I remake
Till I am Timon and Lear
Or that William Blake
Who beat upon the wall
Till truth obeyed his call;

A mind Michael Angelo knew
That can pierce the clouds
Or inspired by frenzy
Shake the dead in their shrouds;
An old man's eagle mind.

– New Poems, 1938

SLIGO

*We have ideas and no passions, but by marriage with a Pollexfen
we have given a tongue to the sea cliffs.*
– John Butler Yeats quoted in *Reveries*, 1915

Ben Bulben

Saint Columba's
Church, Drumcliff

Yeats always maintained that Sligo was the domain and landscape of his poetic imagination. The influence that the people and places of Sligo had on the poet may never be understated, for they sowed in that sensitive and creative mind the seeds of the muse that was to sustain his poetic endeavour for the remainder of his life. It was there that the young poet was first moved to explore the mysteries of the Celtic Sagas and was inspired and excited by the riches contained within the folklore and tales that were related to him by the people of Sligo.

Though the substance and subject matter of Yeats's poetry and other writings were to explore other landscapes, both real and imaginary, Sligo would remain with him throughout his life and in his final poems re-emerge as the spindle in the wheel of his creative and emotional existence as it turned full circle.

> *He that in Sligo at Drumcliff*
> *Set up the old stone Cross,*
> *That red-headed rector in County Down,*
> *A good man on a horse,*
> *Sandymount Corbets, that notable man*
> *Old William Pollexfen,*
> *The smuggler Middleton, Butlers far back,*
> *Half-legendary men.*

– from 'Are You Content' (*New Poems*, 1938)

The Sligo connection was not only on his mother Susan's side. On completing his studies at Dublin University, W.B. Yeats's paternal great-grandfather, John Yeats, took orders in the Church of Ireland, and in 1805, he was sent to the parish of Drumcliff in Sligo, where he remained until his death in 1846. The narrow three-storied rectory he occupied still stands close to Drumcliff Church and the round tower and cross. The family connection, and his desire to be forever in the shadow of Ben Bulben, would lead W.B. Yeats to request that Drumcliff be his final resting place too.

Parson Yeats, according to T. O'Rorke's *History of Sligo*, was a fine scholar; he fished, kept horses and enjoyed convivial company. Indeed when he died he left an outstanding wine bill of the then substantial sum of four hundred pounds for his heirs to pay. He was also a very popular man and highly regarded locally, not only by those of his own religious persuasion. It is said that once, after having been away in Dublin for a protracted period, bonfires that were lit on the orders of the local Catholic priest blazed all over the county in honour of his return.

John Yeats reared a large and academically illustrious family. One son, Thomas, was considered a mathematician of the highest order. The poet's grandfather, William Butler Yeats (a recurring name in the family tree), was educated at Trinity College, Dublin, and was both a notable scholar and a sportsman. In the family tradition he left college and entered the church, becoming a curate in the parish of Moira, Co. Down. He married Jane Corbet of Sandymount in 1836 and was then appointed rector of the parish of Tullylish near Portadown.

His wife gave birth to the poet's father, John Butler Yeats, in 1839. JBY was sent to school at the Atholl Academy in the Isle of Man and it was here that he met George Pollexfen, the son of a shipping magnate and mill owner from Sligo. JBY was later to write in his letters that he was 'intrigued by the slow and tedious' George, who was at once dull enough to freeze conversation and, at the same time, capable of making up long, imaginative stories that would amuse his schoolmates.

Family tradition presumed that John Butler Yeats would become a clergyman. However, a lack of curiosity about God and other theological matters led him to realise that perhaps he should pursue another career. He studied Classics, Metaphysics and Logic at university and later won a prize of ten pounds in Political Economy. On the strength of this money, he set off to visit his friend George in Sligo.

On his home soil, George was a much happier man than JBY remembered from their schooldays. He bubbled with conversation as they walked the coastline around Rosses Point, where the Pollexfens and their close relations, the Middletons, had summer houses. It was during this visit that JBY met George Pollexfen's sister, Susan, to whom he proposed marriage in the summer of 1862. She and the Pollexfens were delighted to be marrying into the grand Butlers of Ormonde – this illustrious family lineage could be traced back to the Anglo-Norman invasion in the late twelfth century – and JBY was, at that time, pursuing a career as a barrister, which his in-laws saw as an honourable and secure profession and an acceptable alternative to life as a clergyman, for he had social status and prospects and was destined to inherit land and an income.

Their marriage took place on September 10th, 1863, at St. John's Church in Sligo. Later, in *Reveries*, Yeats quoted his father as saying, 'We [the Yeatses] have ideas and no passions, but by marriage with a Pollexfen we have given a tongue to the sea cliffs.'

During the night of June 13th, 1865, their first child, William Butler, the poet, was born in Sandymount Avenue, Dublin.

JBY's legal career was, however, short-lived. In 1867 he finally announced his decision to quit the bar and take up art. He took his family to Sligo to stay with his in-laws until he could find suitable accommodation for them in London, where he would attend art school.

By this time Susan's parents, William and Elizabeth Pollexfen, had moved their large family from a towered house on Wine Street in Sligo town – which also served as the head office of the Sligo Steam Navigation Company and from whose tower William Pollexfen could observe the comings and goings of his vessels in the quays below – into a large house and estate called Merville. Susan, then aged twenty-six, had eleven siblings. JBY considered the atmosphere at Merville oppressive and worried about the effect it would have on the young Willie. He later wrote that, whereas the Yeatses were a charming, fun-loving, optimistic and demonstrably affectionate people, the Pollexfens were serious and silent, obsessed with property and position; the two families were the contrast between idealism and cynicism. Writing to his daughter Lily many years later, JBY said of the Yeatses, 'You would be proud to have their blood. They were so clever and so innocent. I never knew and never will know any people so

W.B. Yeats at age seven, with his uncle Fred Pollexfen and Spot the dog, Sligo, 1872

attractive' (*J.B. Yeats: Letters to His Son W.B. Yeats and Others*, 1944). He also wrote that the Pollexfens 'despised literature and poetry as being part of that idleness which they regarded as so calamitous to morals' (*Prodigal Father*, 1978).

JBY lived in the shadow of financial failure for most of his life, and his decision to pursue a career as an artist caused his family great hardship. His views of the Pollexfens might well have been prejudiced by their relative financial success and their disapproval of his career change. Susan Yeats worried about money throughout her life and eventually had four children to care for (two others died in infancy) and a husband who could not sell his paintings. The situation caused unavoidable stress, which no doubt contributed to her suffering a

Knocknashee (Hill of the Sidhe)

series of strokes that caused her to spend the last twelve years of her life as an invalid. When she died on January 3rd, 1900, in London, aged fifty-nine, she had not known the happiness she expected when marrying John and was estranged from the people and places she had loved as a girl. She also didn't live long enough to see the astonishing impact her children would have on the world and the phenomenal impression they would make on literature and art.

Since they could not rely on family finances, the Yeats children had to learn to support themselves, and this they did by various means. Willie wrote and later became a senator. Jack painted and married fellow art student Mary Cottenham White, who came from a well-off family, thus removing himself from impecunity at a stroke. Lily embroidered and Lolly became a printer, founding the Dun Emer Press and later the Cuala Press, which produced many fine prints of Jack's paintings and editions of Willie's poems. When Lily went to New York in 1907 to attend a trade fair of Irish industrial products, she took her debt-ridden father with her. He refused to return to Ireland and remained there until his death in New York City in February, 1922. He is buried at Chester Rural Cemetery in New York State.

An interesting footnote to the relationship between JBY and his in-laws is that once, when the more prosperous W.B. Yeats sent his father a large sum of money for his support in New York, JBY wrote to Lily that though it was like a Yeats to send the money without request and without fuss, it was like the Pollexfens to have had the money to send in the first place.

* * *

Oyster Island Lighthouse, at the mouth
of the channel leading to Sligo Port

From the age of two, W.B. Yeats lived mostly in London. But in 1872, due to a domestic financial crisis, Susan Yeats took her children to her parents' home in Sligo, where they lived from July 1872 until October 1874, when Willie was between the ages of seven and nine. It is considered by many Yeatsian scholars – and admitted by the poet himself – that this period was very influential on his work. To the Yeats children this was a time of great excitement, and to them 'it seemed that everyone in Sligo talked of fairies'. (*Reveries*, 1915.) They found in Sligo a measure of stability, at least compared to their bohemian life in England, and they reacted positively and enthusiastically to their new surroundings, loving the town, its environs, its people and the romantic connection to a sea-faring tradition. Sligo provided young Jack Butler Yeats with inspiration for his art; surrounded by horses, plain fishermen and the rolling seas, he made their depiction his life's work. For Willie, it would be the landscape of his literary imagination.

* * *

The peaceful setting of Sligo Abbey, with the land to the rear slanting down to the Garavogue River, belies a troubled and violent past. The most dramatic and tragic episode in its long history took place on a July night in 1642 when Sir Frederick Hamilton of Manorhamilton in Co. Leitrim, a supporter of Cromwell, avenged the deaths of twenty Protestant soldiers by razing the town of Sligo and putting hundreds of men and women to the sword.

Yeats gives his own creative account of their attack on the

abbey in 'The Curse of the Fires and the Shadows' from his book *The Secret Rose* (1897).

One summer night, when there was peace, a score of Puritan troopers, under the pious Sir Frederick Hamilton, broke through the door of the Abbey of the White Friars at Sligo. As the door fell with a crash they saw a little knot of friars gathered about the altar, their white habits glimmering in the steady light of the holy candles. All the monks were kneeling except the abbot, who stood upon the altar steps with a great brass crucifix in his hand. 'Shoot them!' cried Sir Frederick Hamilton, but nobody stirred, for all were new converts, and feared the candles and the crucifix. For a little while all were silent, and then five troopers, who were the bodyguard of Sir Frederick Hamilton, lifted their muskets, and shot down five of the friars.

Later in 'The Crucifixion of the Outcast' (*The Secret Rose*, 1897), Yeats paints a gruesome picture of the abbey and its surroundings. (A 'gleeman' is a professional entertainer, especially a singer.)

A man, with thin brown hair and a pale face, half ran, half walked, along the road that wound from the south to the town of Sligo. Many called him Cumhal, the son of Cormac, and many called him the Swift, Wild Horse; and he was a gleeman, and he wore a short parti-coloured doublet, and had pointed shoes, and a bulging wallet. Also he was of the blood of the Ernaans, and his birth-place was the Field of Gold; but his eating and sleeping places were the four provinces of Eri, and his abiding place was not upon the ridge of the earth. His eyes strayed from the Abbey tower of the White Friars and the town battlements to a row of crosses which stood out against the sky upon a hill a little to the eastward of the town, and he clenched his fist, and shook it at the crosses. He knew they were not empty, for the birds were fluttering about them; and he thought how, as like as not, just such another vagabond as himself was hanged on one of them; and he muttered: 'If it were hanging or bow-stringing, or stoning or beheading, it would be bad enough. But to have the birds pecking your eyes and the wolves eating your feet!'

… While he spoke, he shivered from head to foot, and the sweat came out upon his face, and he knew not why, for he had looked upon many crosses. He passed over two hills and under the battlemented gate, and then round by a left-hand way to the door of the Abbey. It was studded with great nails, and when he knocked at it, he roused the lay brother who was the porter, and of him he asked a place in the guest-house. Then the lay brother took a glowing turf on a shovel, and led the way to a big and naked outhouse strewn with very dirty rushes; and lighted a rush-candle fixed between two of the stones of the wall, and set the glowing turf upon the hearth and gave him two unlighted sods and a wisp of straw, and showed him a blanket hanging from a nail, and a shelf with a loaf of bread and a jug of water, and a tub in a far corner.

Later, the monks report to the sleeping abbot:

'He is cursing in rhyme, and with two assonances in every line of his curse.'

The abbot pulled his night-cap off and crumpled it in his hands, and the circular brown patch of grey hair in the middle of his bald head looked like the cairn upon Knocknarea, for in Connaught they had not yet aban-doned the ancient tonsure for the style then coming into use. 'If we do not somewhat,' he said, 'he will teach his curses to the children in the street, and the girls spinning at the doors, and to the robbers upon Ben Bulben.'

* * *

Meanwhile the Pollexfens and Middletons conducted their own religious lives in St. John's Church in Sligo town, which was designed by renowned architect Richard Cassels and elevated to cathedral status in the 1960s. It was the venue for family baptisms and weddings and it was here that W.B. Yeats's parents, John Butler Yeats and Susan Pollexfen, were married in 1863. It is here also that both sides of the poet's Sligo ancestry find their final resting places.

The soil of St. John's churchyard was rumoured to have mysterious preservative qualities, preventing the decomposition of bodies buried in it. The aging William Pollexfen personally supervised the construction of the family tomb. Those laid to rest there are celebrated in the Yeats poem 'In Memory of Alfred Pollexfen' (*The Wild Swans at Coole*, 1919).

> *Five-and-twenty years have gone*
> *Since old William Pollexfen*
> *Laid his strong bones down in death*
> *By his wife Elizabeth*
> *In the grey stone tomb he made.*
> *And after twenty years they laid*
> *In that tomb by him and her*
> *His son George, the astrologer;*
> *And Masons drove from miles away*
> *To scatter the Acacia spray*
> *Upon a melancholy man*
> *Who had ended where his breath began.*

The road leading to Inisfree

Inside the church, there is a window dedicated to William and Elizabeth Pollexfen and, near the pulpit, a brass plate in memory of Susan Yeats. It reads:

> *To the memory of*
> *Susan Mary*
> *wife of*
> *John Butler Yeats*
> *and eldest daughter*
> *of the late*
> *William and*
> *Elizabeth Pollexfen*
> *of this town*
> *Born July 13th 1841*
> *Died in London*
> *January 3rd 1900*
> *Erected by her*
> *four children.*

* * *

In the 1870s, enjoying the rewards of a thriving business, the Pollexfens moved into the spacious and comfortable Merville, a large grey eighteenth-century stone house set in grounds of about sixty acres.

The poet's maternal grandfather, William Pollexfen, was renowned for his uncompromising toughness and steely, formidable disposition. There is a story told by Yeats in his autobiography of an instance when it was reported to William

Pollexfen that the keel of one of his boats moored at Rosses Point was damaged. Finding that no one was willing to dive below the waterline, William himself swam down to examine the keel; he emerged a little scratched by the experience but well-informed as to the extent of the damage. It is no wonder that the young and impressionable Yeats would sometimes confuse his apparently all-powerful grandfather with God and the mad King Lear!

He also instilled a fearful respect and admiration in the young man, who was to write in *Reveries* that 'some of my childhood misery was my loneliness, and some of it fear of old William Pollexfen my grandfather. He was never unkind, and I cannot remember that he ever spoke harshly to me, but it was the custom to fear and admire him.'

Yeats later wrote in his autobiography that he remembered little of his childhood but its pain, and that he grew more content with each passing year, feeling that his unhappiness was more due to his own mental state than the influence of others.

Life at Merville was tempered somewhat by his grandmother Elizabeth's presence. Yeats relates in *Reveries* that this mild and gentle woman made it a warm and welcoming home for the family.

At my grandmother's I had learned to love an elaborate house, a garden and trees; and those grey country houses Lissadell, Hazelwood House, and the far, rarely seen tower of Markree, had always called to mind a life set amid natural beauty and the activities of servants and labourers who seemed themselves natural, as bird and tree are natural.

The Pilot House in Rosses Point, which features in 'Memory Harbour' by Jack as well as W.B.'s *The Old Men of the Twilight:* 'The disused pilot house looks out to sea through two round windows like eyes …'

In all of the Pollexfen homes there existed a rigour and a strict code of behaviour, the departure from which was considered wasteful and self-indulgent. It was frowned upon if any member of the family ate between breakfast at 9 a.m. and dinner at 4 p.m. Family members went to bed when it became dark and rose with the first light.

Merville was a rambling, magical demesne for the young Yeats. Here the serious young boy was able to indulge in the more playful pastimes at which his brother Jack excelled. Yeats would play with the dogs and ride the horses for hours; he even remembers attending the hunt one Christmas. The gardens contained apple trees and flower beds and the mesmerising figureheads of two ships. Yeats wrote that 'as a child all my dreams were of ships' (*Memoirs*, 1972).

Sadly it was also at Merville that Robert (Bobbie), the infant brother of W.B. Yeats, died of the croup, aged three, in 1873. The flags of the ships in the harbour were flown at half-mast as a mark of respect.

Merville was also where Willie began his formal education. His aunts, who tried to teach him, considered him lazy and a bad pupil, so his father offered to teach him to read instead of going to church on Sundays. Young Willie's delight soon turned to disappointment when his father flung a book at his son's head in frustration. This prompted Willie to attend church again the following Sunday!

The library at Merville was quite probably the young Yeats's first exposure to books and literature. JBY read out loud to his son and took a deep interest in his education. When he first attended 'proper school', Willie's first lesson was a song, which he sang to his father that evening. His singing was so bad that his father asked the teachers not to teach his son any more songs.

Jack B. Yeats lived with his grandparents in Sligo from 1879 until 1887, long after his brother had left for schools in England and Dublin. Jack was always bottom of the class, but his grandmother didn't mind and thought him 'too kind-hearted to pass the other boys' (*Reveries*, 1915). He was very popular with the locals, whom he drew and sketched; in later life, Willie was to recognise many of the people he met as a child in Jack's paintings.

Jack Butler Yeats. Photograph by Alice Boughton

Just around the corner from Merville is Thornhill, the home of George Pollexfen, Yeats's maternal uncle and erstwhile school friend of his father. It is a small and plain house, but it suited the spartan needs of Uncle George, whose one housekeeper, Mary Battle, was to have a profound effect on the young Yeats.

George had come from Ballina in Co. Mayo in 1882 to fill the place left at the retirement of his own father, William Pollexfen, from his shipping and mill business. 'Young' George was considered fair and mild-mannered, in contrast to his less even-tempered father. As Yeats described in *Reveries*, George was 'a well-to-do, elderly man, [who] lived with no more comfort than when he had set out as a young man'. Even in his early fifties he possessed the habits of a much older person. He was considered a hypochondriac, and he wore weighed woollens as the year progressed to ensure that he carried the exact number of ounces of wool required to keep him warm depending on the season. His fear of illness and of becoming overweight prompted him to keep fit through regular exercise. As an old man, he still had the erect and trim shape of his youth.

He would walk twice each day, after lunch and dinner, to the same gate on the Knocknarea road or, at Rosses Point, to the same rock upon the shore.
– *Reveries*, 1915

George Pollexfen was also an out-and-out pessimist and a harbinger of doom and gloom. He would say to the young W.B. Yeats, 'How very old I shall be in twenty years.' However, his melancholy was at odds with his reputation as a courageous and dashing horseman, and he was considered by many to be the best rider in all of Connaught, racing under the assumed name of 'Paul Hamilton'. People believed he possessed a magical understanding of the ailments of horses, and he was often consulted by owners whose animals would not respond to conventional treatments. He kept a racehorse and a donkey in a field beside the house and would oil their saddles and polish their stirrups frequently over the rest of his life, though he rarely used them.

W.B. Yeats stayed with his uncle at Thornhill from November 1894 to early summer 1895, when the poet was thirty years of age.

It was during this visit that my friendship with my uncle became very close. He never treated me quite as a grown man and had the selfishness of an old bachelor – I remember still with a little resentment that if there was but one kidney with the bacon at breakfast he always took it without apology – and he complained continually of his health.

Yeats goes on to say that he 'began to think of [George's] house very much as one thinks of home. In a sense Sligo has always been my home' (*Memoirs*, 1972).

When George died in 1910, there was a huge funeral in Sligo. This was probably the last public acknowledgement of the importance of the Pollexfens. With the demise of the business, the family's place in the constellations of Sligo public life diminished, and it was not long before their presence faded almost entirely.

George's servant, Mary Battle, was considered to have 'the second sight', which enabled her to perceive things in other dimensions. She is said to have possibly been the cause for George Pollexfen to interest himself in the study of psychic phenomena. Mary also related much to Willie Yeats about the folk tales and customs, habits, beliefs and behaviour of the locals and of the 'faery-host' that was never far away. Yeats himself acknowledges that much of *The Celtic Twilight* (1893) 'is but her daily speech'.

The young Willie Yeats was in awe of the seamen and pilots who made their livelihoods upon the oceans. As a boy, he often made the journey to Sligo during school holidays on one of his grandfather's vessels that sailed from Liverpool. He anticipated the voyages with great excitement and boasted of them joyfully to his schoolmates. He even developed a straight-legged sailor's gait but concealed the fact that he was easily seasick.

When I arrived at the Clarence Basin, Liverpool, on my way to Sligo for my holidays I was among Sligo people. When I was a little boy, an old woman who had come to Liverpool with crates of fowl made me miserable by throwing her arms around me, the moment I had alighted from my cab, and telling the sailor who carried my luggage that she had held me in her arms when I was a baby. The Sailor may have known me almost as well for I was often at Sligo quay to sail my boat; and I came and went once or twice in every year upon the s.s. Sligo *or the s.s.* Liverpool *which belonged to a company that had for directors my grandfather and his partner William Middleton.*

– *Reveries*, 1915

The voyage from Liverpool to Sligo took about thirty hours and was invariably an uncomfortable experience. However, when the ship pulled into Sligo docks, there would be a servant from Merville waiting there to greet the young traveller and escort him back to the house. Young Willie was very popular among the staff at Merville. He was beguiled by their stories and loved listening to them or wandering over the hills with a stable boy for company.

Years later, in 'Under Saturn', Yeats recalled some private vow he had made never to forget his past, his family and the influence they and Sligo had on him as a man and as a poet.

Do not because this day I have grown saturnine
Imagine that lost love, inseparable from my thought
Because I have no other youth, can make me pine;
For how should I forget the wisdom that you brought,
The comfort that you made? Although my wits have gone
On a fantastic ride, my horse's flanks are spurred
By childish memories of an old cross Pollexfen,
And of a Middleton, whose name you never heard,
And of a red-haired Yeats whose looks, although he died
Before my time, seem like a vivid memory.
You heard that labouring man who had served my people. He said
Upon the open road, near to the Sligo quay –
No, no, not said, but cried it out – 'You have come again,
And surely after twenty years it was time to come.'
I am thinking of a child's vow sworn in vain
Never to leave that valley his fathers called their home.

– Michael Robartes and the Dancer, 1921

Elsinore Lodge, now in ruins

The Yeats children were very close to their Pollexfen and Middleton cousins, aunts and uncles, and would visit them at their respective 'holiday' homes at Rosses Point, a small fishing village around ten kilometres north west of Sligo. There they swam, rowed and sailed boats in the mouth of the Garavogue River or between the mainland and Oyster and Coney Islands, which lie just offshore. They also moved freely between the houses of the locals and listened to the stories they told.

The Middletons' home, Elsinore Lodge, was built by a smuggler, John Black, much of whose wealth had derived from his strategic proximity to the hazardous waters between Rosses Point and Oyster Island. The now-ruined house was said to be haunted by the ghosts of smugglers. Legend had it that they would announce their presence by rapping on the window pane. The terrified young Yeats boys would sit at night and listen for the smugglers' spirits to announce their presence on the window.

There were great cellars under the house, for it had been a smuggler's house a hundred years before, and sometimes three loud raps would come upon the drawing-room at sundown, setting all the dogs barking: some dead smuggler giving his accustomed signal. One night I heard them, and later on my sister. A pilot had told me that, after dreaming three times of a treasure buried in my uncle's garden, he had climbed the wall in the middle of the night and begun to dig but grew disheartened 'because there was so much earth'. I told somebody what he had said and was told that it was well he did not find it, for it was guarded by a spirit that looked like a flat-iron.
– Reveries, 1915

Elsinore's last occupant was Henry Middleton, Yeats's eccentric cousin who lived there alone. Yeats and his wife George visited in 1919 and found the gates to be locked. Climbing over the wall, Yeats discovered Henry sitting there dressed in a fine white suit, surrounded by a confused mess, declaring that he was too busy to see anyone. Henry is thought to be Yeats's model for 'John Sherman' in his novel of the same name, and he was immortalised by his cousin in the poem 'Three Songs to the One Burden':

My name is Henry Middleton,
I have a small demesne,
A small forgotten house that's set
On a storm-bitten green.
I scrub its floor and make my bed,
I cook and change my plate,
The post and garden-boy alone
Have keys to my old gate.

– Last Poems, 1939

Some years later, when Yeats visited Rosses Point with his own children, he declined the opportunity to visit his reclusive cousin again. However, his children did try to gain admission to Elsinore but were turned away at the door by a house servant.

* * *

Another favoured spot for smugglers was nearby Dead Man's Point, about which Yeats writes in 'The Old Men of the Twilight' (*The Secret Rose,* 1897). Legend had it that a sailor from foreign lands fell ill and was thought to be dead by his fellow crew members, who were keen to sail off on the next tide. In their haste to be on their way they hurriedly buried him at this place, and in their uncertainty as to his demise, placed a loaf of bread in the grave with him in case he might not be dead after all.

At the place, close to the Dead Man's Point, at the Rosses, where the disused pilot house looks out to sea through two round windows like eyes, a mud cottage stood in the last century. It also was a watchhouse, for a certain old Michael Bruen, who had been a smuggler, and was still the father and grandfather of all smugglers, lived there, and when, after nightfall, a tall French schooner crept over the bay from Roughley, it was his business to hang a horn lantern in the southern window, that the news might travel to Dorren's Island, and thence by another horn lantern, to the village of the Rosses. But for this glimmering of messages, he had little communication with mankind, for he was very old, and had no thought for anything but for the making of his soul, at the foot of the Spanish crucifix of carved oak that hung by his chimney, or bent double over the rosary of stone beads brought to him in a cargo of silks and laces out of France. One night he had watched hour after hour, because a gentle and favourable wind was blowing, and 'La Mere de Misericorde' was much overdue; and he was about to lie down upon his heap of straw, seeing that the dawn was whitening the east, and that the schooner would not dare to round Roughley and come to an anchor after daybreak; when he saw a long line of herons flying slowly from Dorren's Island and towards the pools which lie, half choked with weeds, behind what is called the Second Rosses. He had never before seen herons flying over the sea, for they are shore-keeping birds, and partly because this had startled him out of his drowsiness, and more because the long delay of the schooner kept his cupboard empty, he took down his rusty shot-gun, of which the barrel was tied on with a piece of string, and followed them towards the pools.

Situated on the Perch Rock near Dead Man's Point, the 'Metal Man' navigation aid is dressed in the uniform of a soldier of Napoleon's army, with one hand in his pocket and the other

The Metal Man at Rosses Point

casually pointing towards the Garavogue River and the safe channel that leads into Sligo docks.

A painting by Jack B. Yeats called 'The Metal Man' shows two boys in a small rowing boat waving their hats as they pass. He painted this long after witnessing a small dinghy occupied by two boys getting caught in the powerful currents that swept through the channel known as 'Shrunamile' ('the channel of a thousand currents') that runs between Coney Island and Oyster Island. The Yeats boys themselves often sailed these waters and became familiar with the capricious nature of 'Shrunamile' and the other hazards that lie off the Rosses Point coastline.

Writing about 'Memory Harbour', another painting by his brother that features Rosses Point, W.B. Yeats laments that …

… when I look at my brother's picture houses and anchored ship and distant lighthouse all set close together as in some old map, I recognize in the blue-coated man with the mass of white shirt the pilot I went fishing with, and I am full of disquiet and excitement, and I am melancholy because I have not made more and better verses.
– Reveries, 1915

The Pollexfens, Yeats's other cousins, also owned a house at Rosses Point called Moyle Lodge. This is a plain terraced house with walled gardens facing out across the channel to

Moyle Lodge

Oyster Island and the blinking lighthouse that is situated at the island's western end. It was here that the adolescent Yeats and his uncle George Pollexfen would test their theories of thought transference by concentrating an agreed symbol on the sleeping Mary Battle, the servant with the 'second sight'. Then, the next day, they would ask her to report to them what she had dreamt and they would analyse the results.

Yeats and Pollexfen also experimented with thought transference by walking separately along the sea shore, Willie on the beach and George above on the cliffs. They would each think of a symbol or an image and then compare notes, discovering after a time that they could do this with remarkable accuracy.

The poet wrote in *Reveries* about his other nocturnal activities:

Once when staying with my uncle at Rosses Point where he went for certain months of the year, I called upon a cousin towards midnight and asked him to get his yacht out, for I wanted to find what sea-birds began to stir before dawn. He was indignant and refused; but his elder sister had overheard me and came to the head of the stairs and forbade him to stir, and that so vexed him that he shouted to the kitchen for his sea boots. He came with me in great gloom for he had people's respect, he declared, and nobody so far said he was mad as they said I was, and we got a very sleepy boy out of his bed in the village and set up sail. We put a trawl out, as he thought it would restore his character if he caught some fish, but the wind fell and we were becalmed. I rolled myself in the mainsail and went to sleep for I could sleep anywhere in those days. I was awakened towards dawn to see my cousin and the boy turning out their pockets for money.

A boat was rowing in from Roughley with fish and they wanted to buy
some and pretend they had caught it, but all our pockets were empty.

Through their association with the Middletons, the Yeats boys
were admitted to all the fishermen's cottages in Rosses Point,
and they became familiar with harbour life and the men and
women who lived and worked there. Yeats maintained that it
was through the Middletons that his interest in country stories
was first aroused. He heard them in the cottages around Rosses
Point and recognised, at an early age, the value of storytelling.

All the well-known families had their stories and how terrible it would
be to go away and die where nobody would know my story.
– *Reveries*, 1915

He also writes in *Reveries* of his great-aunt Micky's house in
the hamlet of Cregg near Rosses Point.

There was a little square two-storeyed house covered with creepers and
looking out upon a garden where the box borders were larger than any
I had ever seen, and where I saw for the first time the crimson streak of
the gladiolus and awaited its blossom with excitement. Under one gable
a dark thicket of small trees made a shut-in mysterious place, where one
played and believed that something was going to happen. My great-aunt
Micky lived there. Micky was not her right name for she was Mary Yeats
and her father had been my great-grandfather, John Yeats, who had been
rector of Drumcliff, a few miles further off, and died in 1847. She was a
spare, high-coloured, elderly woman and had the oldest-looking cat I had
ever seen, for its hair had grown into matted locks of yellowy white. She

farmed and had one old man-servant, but could not have farmed at all, had not neighbouring farmers helped to gather in the crops, in return for the loan of her farm implements and 'out of respect for the family,' for as Johnny MacGurk, the Sligo barber said to me, 'The Yeats's were always very respectable.'

The Yeats ancestry is also closely linked with the nearby village of Drumcliff, once the site of a monastic settlement founded by St. Colmcille. The poet's great grandfather, John Yeats, was rector at St. Columba's Church in Drumcliff from 1805 until 1846, as recalled in 'Are You Content':

> *I call on those that call me son,*
> *Grandson, or great-grandson,*
> *On uncles, aunts, great-uncles or great-aunts,*
> *To judge what I have done.*
> *Have I, that put it into words,*
> *Spoilt what old loins have sent?*
> *Eyes spiritualised by death can judge,*
> *I cannot, but I am not content.*

> *He that in Sligo at Drumcliff*
> *Set up the old stone Cross,*
> *That red-headed rector in County Down,*
> *A good man on a horse,*
> *Sandymount Corbets, that notable man*
> *Old William Pollexfen*
> *The smuggler Middleton, Butlers far back,*
> *Half legendary men.*

The high cross
at Drumcliff

Infirm and aged I might stay
In some good company,
I who have always hated work,
Smiling at the sea,
Or demonstrate in my own life
What Robert Browning meant
By an old hunter talking with Gods;
But I am not content.

– New Poems, 1938

Of course the most significant feature of Drumcliff is that W.B. Yeats himself is buried there, in the graveyard of St. Columba's. When he died in Roquebrune-Cap-Martin, France, in January 1939, he was, in accordance with his wishes, initially buried at the local cemetery. His desire was that his body remain there for a year or so and then be exhumed and taken to Ireland and buried at Drumcliff. This unusual request was thwarted by the outbreak of the Second World War, and it wasn't until 1948 that moves were made to exhume his remains. There was some controversy about this at the time as it was discovered that the poet's remains had actually been moved by cemetery employees much earlier than planned and placed in an ossuary with those of other people, as is the custom in parts of Europe. Eventually, the remains were identified and re-coffined.

Then, on September 8th, 1948, amidst great pomp and ceremony, the coffin was removed and driven to Villefranche with a military guard of honour and draped in the Irish flag. There it was carried onto the Irish naval vessel *Macha* and transported to Galway. In the early morning of September 17ᵗʰ, the ship was greeted by Yeats's widow, George, his children, Michael and Anne, and his brother Jack, and they accompanied the cortège to Sligo, where it was received by an Irish military guard of honour. The Yeats family had declined the offer of a state funeral.

Later that day, in the quiet, peaceful, sycamore-fringed churchyard in Drumcliffe, the body of W.B. Yeats was re-interred in a simple, fern-lined grave as he had requested. His headstone is inscribed with the last three tantalising lines of his poem 'Under Ben Bulben'.

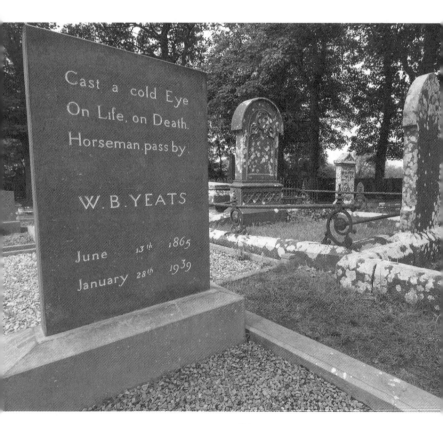

Under bare Ben Bulben's head
In Drumcliff churchyard Yeats is laid.
An ancestor was rector there
Long years ago; a church stands near,
By the road an ancient Cross.
No marble, no conventional phrase;
On limestone quarried near the spot
By his command these words are cut:
Cast a cold eye
On life, on death.
Horseman, pass by!

– Last Poems, 1939

George, the poet's wife, is also buried at Drumcliff. The doors of St. Columba's Church bear handles in the shape of swans, commemorating the poet's frequent use of the swan in his poetic imagery.

* * *

Yeats was twenty-nine years old when he first visited Lissadell House on the shores of Sligo Bay in November 1894 at the invitation of the Gore-Booth family, who had begun to admire his work as a poet. The Gore-Booths had always been at the cutting edge of social and political reform and were associated with progressive farming, industry and landlord-tenant relations.

During the Famine, Sir Robert Gore-Booth, the then owner

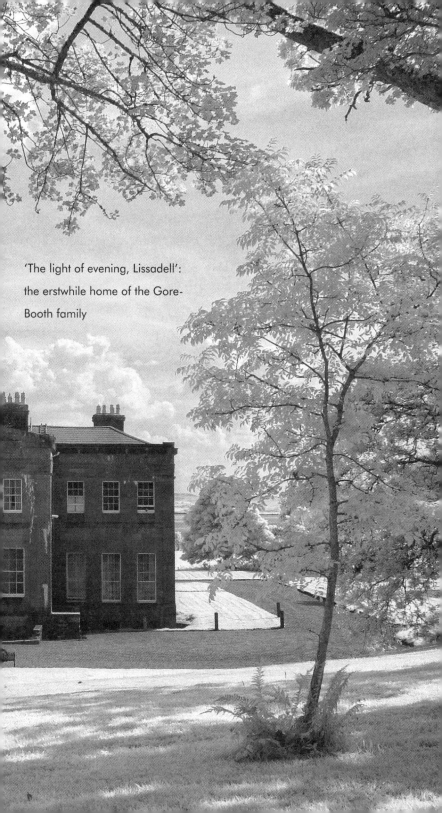

'The light of evening, Lissadell':
the erstwhile home of the Gore-
Booth family

and builder of the house, set up food supplies for starving tenants. He also gave financial aid to more than 250 tenants to emigrate to Canada or elsewhere. Sir Robert's grandson, Sir Josslyn, actively supported the co-operative movement, which sought to distribute agricultural earnings fairly and evenly amongst the producers, and there was a school on the estate for the children of the Lissadell tenants, paid for by the family. Lady Georgina Gore-Booth ran a school of needlework to provide employment for local women.

Yeats always seemed to secretly desire the status conferred by being part of the Anglo-Irish ascendancy. His own descent from clergymen and businessmen was not quite the same and, though he grew to be familiar with the 'gentry' and their houses and ways, he was forever intimidated by them.

In my childhood I had seen on clear days from the hill above my grandmother's house or from the carriage if our drive was towards Ben Bulben or from the smooth grass hill of Rosses the grey stone walls of Lissadell among its trees. We were merchant people of the town. No matter how rich we grew, no matter how many thousands a year our mills or our ships brought in, we could never be 'county', nor indeed had we any desire to be so. We would meet on grand juries those people in the great houses – Lissadell among its woods, Hazelwood House by the lake's edge, and Markree Castle encircled by wood after wood – and we would speak no malicious gossip and knew ourselves respected in turn, but the long-settled habit of Irish life set up a wall.

– Memoirs, 1972

The Gore-Booth daughters, Constance and Eva, were renowned throughout Sligo for their feats of daring and horsemanship. Constance became politically active during her relatively short life. She was a founder member of Na Fianna Éireann, a boy scout movement with nationalist tendencies. During the 1916 Rising in Dublin she held a senior position and, upon capture, was tried and sentenced to death. Her sentence was commuted to life imprisonment and she was incarcerated in an English jail.

'On A Political Prisoner'

When long ago I saw her ride
Under Ben Bulben to the meet,
The beauty of her country-side
With all youth's lonely wildness stirred,
She seemed to have grown clean and sweet
Like any rock-bred, sea-borne bird:

Sea-borne, or balanced in the air
When first it sprang out of the nest
Upon some lofty rock to stare
Upon the cloudy canopy,
While under its storm-beaten breast
Cried out the hollows of the sea.

– Michael Robartes and the Dancer, 1921

Yeats was fond of Constance in their youth but grew less so as the years went on, particularly when she helped set up a rival company to his Abbey Theatre. She married a Polish count, an

Countess Markievicz, née Constance Gore-Booth

artist named Casimir de Markievicz, who painted the life-size murals on the walls of the dining room at Lissadell House. She died in 1927.

Constance's sister Eva, with whom Yeats had a warmer and more enduring relationship, became involved in the suffragette movement in England. Encouraged by Yeats, she wrote and published numerous volumes of poetry and prose as well as plays. Eva was also destined to live a short life and died less than a year before her sister, in 1926.

'In Memory of Eva Gore-Booth and Con Markievicz'

The light of evening, Lissadell,
Great windows, open to the south,
Two girls in kimonos, both
Beautiful, one a gazelle.
But a raving autumn shears
Blossom from the summer's wreath;
The older is condemned to death,
Pardoned, drags out lonely years
Conspiring among the ignorant.
I know not what the younger dreams –
Some vague Utopia – and she seems,
When withered old and skeleton-gaunt,
An image of such politics.
Many a time I think to seek
One or the other out and speak
Of that old Georgian mansion, mix
pictures of the mind, recall
That table and the talk of youth,
Two girls in silk kimonos, both
Beautiful, one a gazelle.

– The Winding Stair, 1933

On the northern shore of Drumcliff Bay, just beyond the erstwhile Gore-Booth estate, is Lissadell Strand, a shallow spit of beach that runs into Drumcliff Bay with views of the Ox Mountains in the distant south and Blackrock Lighthouse and Coney Island and Rosses Point in between.

'The Man Who Dreamed of Faeryland'

He wandered by the sands of Lissadell;
His mind ran all on money cares and fears,
And he had known at last some prudent years
Before they heaped his grave under the hill;
But while he passed before a plashy place,
A lug-worm with its grey and muddy mouth
Sang that somewhere to north or west or south
There dwelt a gay, exulting, gentle race
Under the golden or the silver skies;
That if a dancer stayed his hungry foot
It seemed the sun and moon were in the fruit:
And at that singing he was no more wise.

– *Poems*, 1895

* * *

Ben Bulben

The extent to which Ben Bulben fired Yeats's creativity cannot be overestimated. The mysterious limestone flat-topped mountain features frequently in his writings, whether prose or poem. It contained all that the poet's fertile imagination required to inspire a landscape upon which his characters play their parts.

A little north of the town of Sligo, on the southern side of Ben Bulben, some hundreds of feet above the plain, is a small white square in the limestone. No mortal has ever touched it with his hand, no sheep or goat has ever browsed grass beside it. There is no more unaccessible place upon the earth, and to an anxious consideration few more encircled by terror. It is the door of faeryland. In the middle of night it swings open, and the unearthly troop rushes out. All night the gay rabble sweep to and fro across the land, invisible to all, unless perhaps where, in some more than commonly 'gentle' place – Drumcliff or Dromahair, the night-capped heads of 'faery-doctors' or 'cow-doctors' may be thrust from their doors to see what mischief the 'gentry' are doing.

– 'Kidnappers' (*The Celtic Twilight*, 1893)

Another enchanted mountain to feature in Yeats's work is Lugnagall. In 'The Man Who Dreamed of Faeryland' (*Poems*, 1895), he evokes all the mystery of its misted slopes.

He slept under the hill of Lugnagall;
And might have known at last unhaunted sleep
Under that cold and vapour-turbaned steep,
Now that the earth had taken man and all:
Did not the worms that spired about his bones

Proclaim with that unwearied, reedy cry
That God has laid His fingers on the sky,
That from those fingers glittering summer runs
Upon the dancer by the dreamless wave.
Why should those lovers that no lovers miss
Dream, until God burn Nature with a kiss?
The man has found no comfort in the grave.

The waters were just as inspirational to Yeats as the mountains. Glencar Waterfall, across the border from Sligo in County Leitrim, is one of the locations most associated with the poet.

'The Stolen Child'

Where dips the rocky highland
Of Sleuth Wood in the lake,
There lies a leafy island
Where flapping herons wake
The drowsy water-rats;
There we've hid our faery vats,
Full of berries
And of reddest stolen cherries.
Come away, O human child!
To the waters and the wild
With a faery, hand in hand,
For the world's more full of weeping than you can understand.

Where the wave of moonlight glosses
The dim grey sands with light,
Far off by furthest Rosses

Glencar Waterfall

We foot it all the night,

Weaving olden dances,

Mingling hands and mingling glances

Till the moon has taken flight;

To and fro we leap

And chase the frothy bubbles,

While the world is full of troubles

And is anxious in its sleep.

Come away, O human child!

To the waters and the wild

With a faery, hand in hand,

For the world's more full of weeping than you can understand.

Where the wandering water gushes

From the hills above Glen-Car,

In pools among the rushes

That scarce could bathe a star,

We seek for slumbering trout

And whispering in their ears

Give them unquiet dreams;

Leaning softly out

From ferns that drop their tears

Over the young streams.

Come away, O human child!

To the waters and the wild

With a faery, hand in hand,

For the world's more full of weeping than you can understand.

– Poems, 1895

* * *

The wind has bundled up the clouds high over Knocknarea,
And thrown the thunder on the stones for all that Maeve can say.
Angers that are like noisy clouds have set our hearts abeat;
But we have all bent low and low and kissed the quiet feet
Of Cathleen, the daughter of Houlihan.

– from 'Red Hanrahan's Song about Ireland'
(*In the Seven Woods*, 1903)

On a clear day, the view from the top of Knocknarea (Hill of the Kings) is breathtaking. It is capped by the legendary Queen Maeve's Cairn, which dates to about 3,000 B.C. and is said to be the grave of the wild queen of Connaught. Yeats was

In a cleft that's christened Alt
Under broken stone I halt
At the bottom of a pit
That broad noon has never lit,
And shout a secret to the stone.

– from 'Man and the Echo' (*Last Poems*, 1939)

continually fascinated by both the legend of Queen Maeve and Knocknarea.

'The Hosting of the Sidhe'

The host is riding from Knocknarea
And over the grave of Clooth-na-Bare;
Caoilte tossing his burning hair,
And Niamh calling Away, come away:
Empty your heart of its mortal dream.
The winds awaken, the leaves whirl round,
Our cheeks are pale, our hair is unbound,
Our breasts are heaving, our eyes are agleam,
Our arms are waving, our lips are apart;
And if any gaze on our rushing band,
We come between him and the deed of his hand,
We come between him and the hope of his heart.
The host is rushing twixt night and day,
And where is there hope or deed as fair?
Caoilte tossing his burning hair,
And Niamh calling Away, come away.

– from *The Wind Among the Reeds,* 1899

The Alt Cleft, also known as The Glen, located close to the base of Knocknarea, is a rarified place teeming with vegetation and birdsong and tall beech trees. This cathedral-like place inspired Yeats's poem 'Man and the Echo'.

In a cleft that's christened Alt
Under broken stone I halt

At the bottom of a pit
That broad noon has never lit,
And shout a secret to the stone.

– Last Poems, 1939

Also close to Knocknarea is the large collection of megalithic burial mounds at Carrowmore, some of the tombs dating to the fifth century B.C. Yeats celebrated the legend that the ancient tribe of the Firbolg buried their dead here in his epic poem 'The Wanderings of Oisin'.

Caoilte, and Conan, and Finn were there,
When we followed a deer with our baying hounds,
With Bran, Sceolan, and Lomair,
And passing the Firbolgs' burial-mounds,
Came to the cairn-heaped grassy hill
Where passionate Maeve is stony-still;

– The Wanderings of Oisin and Other Poems, 1889

Legend has it that Lough Gill gets its name from Gile, the daughter of a chieftain who once ruled over a city that, like Atlantis or Hy-Brasil, lies submerged deep beneath its waters. Gile's tragic death prompted her nurse to weep until her tears filled the valley and formed the lake. W.B. Yeats was drawn to the lake's beauty and the mysteries of its wooded shores, its islands and its ancient history and legends. During the winter of 1881–1882, when he was sixteen years old, Lough Gill froze over and the Yeats children learned to skate.

High above the lough is a huge chunk of limestone called

Knocknarea

Dooney Rock, set among woods of beech and pine and home to a great variety of rare flora and fauna. Yeats visited the rock on many occasions as a boy and was drawn to its seclusion and quiet.

'The Fiddler of Dooney'

When I play on my fiddle in Dooney,
Folk dance like a wave of the sea;
My cousin is priest in Kilvarnet,
My brother in Mocharabuiee.

I passed my brother and cousin:
They read in their books of prayer;
I read in my book of songs
I bought at the Sligo fair.

When we come at the end of time
To Peter sitting in state,
He will smile on the three old spirits,
But call me first through the gate;

For the good are always the merry,
Save by an evil chance,
And the merry love the fiddle,
And the merry love to dance:

And when the folk there spy me,
They will all come up to me,
With 'Here is the fiddler of Dooney!'
And dance like a wave of the sea.

– The Wind Among the Reeds, 1899

The most famous of Lough Gill's islands, of course, is Innisfree, the inspiration for one of Yeats's best-known and best-loved poems. As a young man, he dreamed of living there, as he describes in *Reveries*:

> *My father had read to me some passage out of* Walden *[by Thoreau] and I planned to live some day in a cottage on a little island called Inisfree, and Inisfree was opposite Slish Wood where I meant to sleep ... I do not remember whether I chose the island because of its beauty or for the sake of a story, but I was twenty-two or three before I gave up the dream.*
>
> *I set out from Sligo about six in the evening, walking slowly, for it was an evening of great beauty; but though I was well into Slish Wood by bed-time, I could not sleep, not from the discomfort of the dry rock I had chosen for my bed, but from my fear of the wood-ranger ... However, I could watch my island in the early dawn and notice the order of the cries of the birds.*
>
> *I came home next day unimaginably tired and sleepy, having walked some thirty miles partly over rough and boggy ground. For months afterwards, if I alluded to my walk, my uncle's general servant would go into fits of laughter. She believed I had spent the night in a different fashion and had invented the excuse to deceive my uncle, and would say to my great embarrassment, for I was as prudish as an old maid, 'And you had good right to be fatigued.'*

Later, in *The Trembling of the Veil* (1922), he returns to this idea and the inspiration for the poem:

> *I had still the ambition, formed in Sligo in my teens, of living in imitation of Thoreau on Innisfree, a little island in Lough Gill, and when*

walking through Fleet Street very homesick I heard a little tinkle of water and saw a fountain in a shop-window which balanced a little ball upon its jet, and began to remember lake water. From the sudden remembrance came my poem 'Innisfree', my first lyric with anything in its rhythm of my own music. I had begun to loosen rhythm as an escape from rhetoric and from that emotion of the crowd that rhetoric brings, but I only understood vaguely and occasionally that I must for my special purpose use nothing but the common syntax. A couple of years later I could not have written that first line with its conventional archaism – 'Arise and go' – nor the inversion of the last stanza.

There is a recording, made by the BBC, of Yeats reciting this poem and talking briefly about its origin. His seventy-two-year-old voice almost chants or sings the lyrics, and he unapologetically refuses to recite the poem as if it were prose as, he acknowledges, he 'had a difficult time shaping it into verse'.

'The Lake Isle of Innisfree'

I will arise and go now, and go to Innisfree,
And a small cabin build there, of clay and wattles made:
Nine bean-rows will I have there, a hive for the honey-bee,
And live alone in the bee-loud glade.

And I shall have some peace there, for peace comes dropping slow,
Dropping from the veils of the morning to where the cricket sings;
There midnight's all a glimmer, and noon a purple glow,
And evening full of the linnet's wings.

Lough Gill

I will arise and go now, for always night and day
I hear lake water lapping with low sounds by the shore;
While I stand on the roadway, or on the pavements grey,
I hear it in the deep heart's core.

– Poems, 1895

Hazelwood House, designed by Richard Cassels – he of Leinster House, the Rotunda and Powerscourt House as well as St. John's Cathedral in Sligo – is situated on the romantically named Half-Moon Bay on Lough Gill. It was once owned by the wealthy Wynne family, and Yeats was a frequent visitor. There is no doubt that the poet was deeply impressed by the demesne and its beauty and, though there is no evidence to support the theory, this place is widely associated with the 'Hazelwood' of his well-known poem 'The Song of Wandering Aengus'.

I went out to the hazel wood,
Because a fire was in my head,
And cut and peeled a hazel wand,
And hooked a berry to a thread;
And when white moths were on the wing,
And moth–like stars were flickering out,
I dropped the berry in a stream
And caught a little silver trout.

When I had laid it on the floor
I went to blow the fire aflame,
But something rustled on the floor,
And some one called me by my name:

It had become a glimmering girl
With apple blossom in her hair
Who called me by my name and ran
And faded through the brightening air.

Though I am old with wandering
Through hollow lands and hilly lands,
I will find out where she has gone,
And kiss her lips and take her hands;
And walk among long dappled grass,
And pluck till time and times are done
The silver apples of the moon,
The golden apples of the sun.

– *The Wind Among the Reeds*, 1899

* * *

W.B. wasn't the only Yeats whose creative prowess attracted worldwide acclaim. His father, John Butler Yeats, may have achieved much success posthumously, but his work could not support him and his family while he was alive. It is Willie's brother Jack who became the better-known artist during his lifetime. Jack spent a great deal of his childhood in Sligo living with his grandparents. The inlet of Ballisodare Bay, where an annual horse race is held, was the inspiration for his famous watercolour 'Will He Catch Them?' It is not difficult to imagine that his brother, too, was inspired by the sands of Ballisodare when he wrote the epic poem 'Cuchulain's Fight with the Sea'.

John Butler Yeats, photographed by Alice Boughton

A man came slowly from the setting sun,
To Emer, raddling raiment in her dun,
And said, 'I that am swineherd whom you bid
Go watch the road between the wood and tide,
But now I have no need to watch it more.'...

'The Red Branch camp in a great company
Between wood's rim and the horses of the sea.
Go there, and light a camp-fire at wood's rim;
But tell your name and lineage to him
Whose blade compels, and wait till they have found
Some feasting man that the same oath has bound.'...

Cuchulain stirred,
Stared on the horses of the sea, and heard
The cars of battle and his own name cried;
And fought with the invulnerable tide.

– Poems, 1895

Yeats's great-uncle, William Middleton, lived at Avena House, which is located just off the main street in Ballisodare close to the mills that stood on either side of the gushing Ballisodare River. (William also owned Elsinore Lodge at Rosses Point.) W.B. Yeats visited his uncle and cousins frequently and was very receptive to the folk- and fairytales told to him by their employees. One such person was Paddy Flynn, William Middleton's gardener.

At Ballisodare an event happened that brought me back to the super-
stitions of my childhood. I do not know when it was, for the events of this

period have as little sequence as those of childhood. I was staying with cousins at Avena house, a young man a few years older, and a girl of my own age and perhaps her sister who was a good deal older. My girl cousin had often told me of strange sights she had seen at Ballisodare or Rosses. An old woman three or four feet in height and leaning on a stick had once come to the window and looked in at her, and sometimes she would meet people on the road who would say 'How is so-and-so,' naming some member of her family, and she would know, though she could not explain how, that they were not people of this world. Once she had lost her way in a familiar field, and when she found it again the silver mounting on a walking-stick belonging to her brother which she carried, had vanished. An old woman in the village said afterwards, 'You have good friends amongst them, and the silver was taken instead of you.'

– Reveries, 1915

Yeats goes on to describe the experience of a servant hearing loud footsteps in the house and seeing the bases of some trees all ablaze with light. He was with his cousins and their friends when …

… suddenly we all saw a light moving over the river where there is a great rush of waters. It was like a very brilliant torch. A moment later the girl saw a man coming towards us who disappeared in the water. I kept asking myself if I could be deceived. Perhaps, after all, though it seemed impossible, someone was walking in the water with a torch. But we could see a small light low down on Knocknarea seven miles off, and it began to move upward over the mountain slope. I timed it on my watch and in five minutes it reached the summit, and I, who have often climbed the mountain, knew that no human footstep was so speedy.

From that on I wandered about raths and faery hills and questioned old women and old men.

Ballisodare's closest association with Yeats is through one of his best-known and best-loved poems, 'Down by the Salley Gardens'. It is said that he was walking near the river in Ballisodare when he heard an old woman who was sitting outside her cottage sing a song, and that he borrowed part of the song to make the poem. 'Salley' is the name given to willows in many parts of Ireland; it is an anglicisation of the Irish word for willow, which is 'saileach', and the Latin 'salix'. The willows were used for basket-making and for roofing, and it was not unusual to find 'salley gardens' growing throughout Ireland.

The Hawk's Rock

'Down by the salley Gardens'

Down by the salley gardens my love and I did meet;
She passed the salley gardens with little snow-white feet.
She bid me take love easy, as the leaves grow on the tree;
But I, being young and foolish, with her would not agree.

In a field by the river my love and I did stand,
And on my leaning shoulder she laid her snow-white hand.
She bid me take life easy, as the grass grows on the weirs;
But I was young and foolish, and now am full of tears.

– Poems, 1895

THE WEST

For all things the delighted eye now sees
Were loved by him; the old storm-broken trees
That cast their shadows upon road and bridge;
The tower set on the stream's edge;
The ford where drinking cattle make a stir
Nightly, and startled by that sound
The water-hen must change her ground;
He might have been your heartiest welcomer.

– from 'In Memory of Major Robert Gregory'
(*The Wild Swans at Coole*, 1919)

Lady Augusta Gregory

One of the most fortuitous meetings in Yeats's life took place in August 1896 at Tulira Castle near Ardrahan, Co. Galway. Yeats and his English poet friend Arthur Symons were on a hiking tour of the west of Ireland, visiting the Aran Islands, Sligo and Galway and staying with Edward Martyn at this grand neo-Gothic stately residence. Symons was then the editor of *Savoy* magazine, to which Martyn was a contributor. While staying there a neighbour, Lady Augusta Gregory, paid them a visit. Gregory and Yeats had met briefly before at a literary gathering in London, and Gregory knew of Yeats's work. On this occasion she invited him to her home some four miles away, which is how Yeats first came to visit Coole Park.

A glimpse of a long vista of trees, over an undergrowth of clipped laurels, seen for a moment as the outside car approached her house on my first visit, is a vivid memory … In later years I was to know the edges of that lake better than any spot on earth, to know it in all the changes of the seasons, to find there always some new beauty.

– The Trembling of the Veil, 1922

That first visit admitted Yeats into the world of the Irish landed gentry and provided him with access to an environment that could and would sustain his work and life to an unimaginable degree. In Lady Gregory he found a friend and patron who would furnish him with the space, time, environment and finances he needed to let his creativity flourish. He

The trees of Coole Park

also found a collaborator whose guidance he came to admire and respect over the decades.

For twenty years I spent two or three months there in every year. Because of those summers, because of that money [loaned to him by Lady Gregory], *I was able through the greater part of my working life to write without thought of anything but the beauty and the utility of what I wrote.*
– *Autobiographies*, 1927

Coole Park was purchased in the late eighteenth century by Robert Gregory, who had made a considerable fortune as director and chairman of the East India Company. He set about having a large house built there with driveways and gardens, stables and outbuildings, features that remain today.

Isabella Augusta Persse had grown up in Roxborough House near Kilchreest, Co. Galway, which was destroyed in 1922 during the Irish Civil War. In 1880, when she was twenty-eight, she married Sir William Gregory, son of Robert, who was then sixty-three, and became Lady Gregory. After the deaths of Sir William and the couple's son, also called Robert, the estate was placed under a huge financial strain and finally sold to the Ministry of Lands and Agriculture in 1927. Lady Gregory managed to remain in Coole Park until her death in 1932 only by agreeing to pay one hundred pounds per annum to the State. Tragically in 1941 the house was demolished by a local builder for its stone. What remains today is the foundation on which it once stood. The stables, the great woods, the walled garden with its vast variety of plants and trees, the trails and the lake still remain.

* * *

In late June 1897, a year after Yeats's first visit to Coole Park, he was once again staying with Edward Martyn at Tulira Castle. Yeats was both physically and emotionally exhausted after a sordid period of rejection by Maud Gonne. Martyn, Gregory and Yeats went to visit a French poet who lived near the entrance to Kinvara Bay.

On the sea coast at Duras, a few miles from Coole, an old French count, Florimond de Basterot, lived for certain months in every year. Lady Gregory and I talked over my project of an Irish Theatre looking out upon the lawn of his house, watching a large flock of ducks that was always gathered for his arrival from Paris … I told her that I had given up my project because it was impossible to get the few pounds necessary for a start in little halls, and she promised to collect or give the money necessary. That was her first great service to the Irish intellectual movement.

– The Trembling of the Veil, 1922

This was a crucial moment in the emergence of the Irish literary revival. Without Lady Gregory's encouragement, her sound pragmatic guidance and management skills, Yeats might have abandoned his hopes then, dashed upon the rocks of indifference and penury. But that summer she provided the love-sick Yeats with even more distraction.

Lady Gregory, seeing that I was ill, brought me from cottage to cottage to gather folk-belief, tales of the faeries, and the like, and wrote down herself what we had gathered, considering that this work, in which one

Yeats, Lady Gregory and Robert Gregory, and Michael Curley
(the piper), who was a regular visitor to Coole Park.

let others talk, and walked about the fields so much, would lie, to use a
country phrase, 'very light upon the mind'.
   – *The Trembling of the Veil*, 1922

Coole Park provided Yeats with the stability he lacked else-
where; it was an antidote to the wanderings of his pilgrim
soul throughout Europe and America in pursuit of his art
and his passions. His relationship with Lady Gregory was a
symbiotic one, she providing a steady, nurturing hand, and
he providing the spark of inspiration and a burning desire
to revolutionise the Irish literary scene. When he received a
letter from Lady Gregory's son Robert in 1909 telling him of
her illness, Yeats wrote:

I thought my mother was ill and that my sister was asking me to come
at once: then I remembered that my mother died years ago and that

more than kin was at stake. She has been to me mother, friend, sister and brother. I cannot realize the world without her – she brought to my wavering thoughts steadfast nobility. All day the thought of losing her is like a conflagration in the rafters. Friendship is all the house I have.
– *Memoirs*, 1972

Yeats's extended stays at Coole Park, sometimes lasting months, eventually grated on the estate's heir, Robert, who was married and had children. Into his inherited home came a continuous trail of his mother's friends and their acquaintances including George Moore, George Russell (Æ), Douglas Hyde, Iseult Gonne, George Bernard Shaw and J.M. Synge, many of whose initials are carved on the 'Autograph Tree', a grand copper beech that still stands within the walled garden. At one point Robert removed Yeats from the master bedroom and banned all guests from accessing the wine cellar.

Eventually Yeats found his own home nearby at Ballylee; nevertheless, he and the others continued to visit. The house, its seven woods and its people are invoked in numerous Yeats poems, such as 'Coole Park, 1929' and 'The Wild Swans at Coole'.

'The Wild Swans at Coole'

The trees are in their autumn beauty,
The woodland paths are dry,
Under the October twilight the water
Mirrors a still sky;
Upon the brimming water among the stones
Are nine-and-fifty swans.

The autograph tree at Coole Park

The nineteenth autumn has come upon me
Since I first made my count;
I saw, before I had well finished,
All suddenly mount
And scatter wheeling in great broken rings
Upon their clamorous wings.

I have looked upon those brilliant creatures,
And now my heart is sore.
All's changed since I, hearing at twilight,
The first time on this shore,
The bell-beat of their wings above my head,
Trod with a lighter tread.

Unwearied still, lover by lover,
They paddle in the cold

Companionable streams or climb the air;
Their hearts have not grown old;
Passion or conquest, wander where they will,
Attend upon them still.

But now they drift on the still water,
Mysterious, beautiful;
Among what rushes will they build,
By what lake's edge or pool
Delight men's eyes when I awake some day
To find they have flown away?

– The Wild Swans at Coole, 1919

'Coole Park, 1929'

I meditate upon a swallow's flight,
Upon an aged woman and her house,
A sycamore and lime tree lost in night
Although that western cloud is luminous,
Great works constructed there in nature's spite
For scholars and for poets after us,
Thoughts long knitted into a single thought,
A dance-like glory that those walls begot.

There Hyde before he had beaten into prose
That noble blade the Muses buckled on,
There one that ruffled in a manly pose
For all his timid heart, there that slow man,
That meditative man, John Synge, and those
Impetuous men, Shawe-Taylor and Hugh Lane,
Found pride established in humility,
A scene well set and excellent company.

They came like swallows and like swallows went,
And yet a woman's powerful character
Could keep a swallow to its first intent;
And half a dozen in formation there,
That seemed to whirl upon a compass-point,
Found certainty upon the dreaming air,
The intellectual sweetness of those lines
That cut through time or cross it withershins.

Here, traveller, scholar, poet, take your stand
When all those rooms and passages are gone,
When nettles wave upon a shapeless mound

And saplings root among the broken stone,
And dedicate – eyes bent upon the ground,
Back turned upon the brightness of the sun
And all the sensuality of the shade –
A moment's memory to that laurelled head.

– The Winding Stair, 1933

Today Coole Park is open to the public, and though the house has gone, as Yeats predicted, the grounds are still mysterious and enthralling. Walks throughout the estate are marked and there is an information centre close to the entrance. The avenues of trees still stand, as does the walled garden in which plants from all over the world are grown in keeping with the horticultural eclecticism of the first branch of the Gregory family to live here.

* * *

II. My House

An ancient bridge, and a more ancient tower,
A farmhouse that is sheltered by its wall,
An acre of stony ground,
Where the symbolic rose can break in flower,
Old ragged elms, old thorns innumerable,
The sound of the rain or sound
Of every wind that blows;
The stilted water-hen
Crossing stream again
Scared by the splashing of a dozen cows;

Thoor Ballylee

A winding stair, a chamber arched with stone,
A grey stone fireplace with an open hearth,
A candle and written page.
Il Penseroso's *Platonist toiled on*
In some like chamber, shadowing forth
How the daemonic rage
Imagined everything.
Benighted travellers
From markets and from fairs
Have seen his midnight candle glimmering.

– The Tower, 1928

By 1916 Yeats had been seduced and absorbed by the gentility and refinements of the literary and artistic world that revolved around Lady Gregory's estate. Still, he craved rootedness and eventually found it in a ruined square Norman keep on the Gregory estates on the bank of the Streamstown River. He was excited by the rawness of the tower and the deep-rooted folklore that dwelt in and around it, as well as its proximity to Coole Park and Edward Martyn's Tulira Castle and its easy access to the railway that stopped at Gort.

On May 16th, 1917, Yeats became the official owner of Ballylee Castle for the sum of thirty-five pounds, and he immediately set about appointing the Dublin architect William Scott and local builder Thomas Rafferty to renovate. It would be the summer of 1919 before he and George, whom he married in October 1917, were able to finally move in, with delays caused by a wartime shortage of materials. The ironwork was made at Burke's Forge in Gort and the furniture by Gort carpenter Patrick Connolly.

Renamed Thoor Ballylee, work continued on the tower into the early 1920s. In a letter to his friend John Quinn in June 1922, Yeats described the renovations:

Our bedroom is upstairs in the Castle and is a delight to us, and the third floor which is to be my study is almost ready. Our dining room on the ground floor was finished three years ago. This is the first year in which we have been able to sleep in the Castle itself. We have added an extra cottage, which is ultimately to be a garage, though not for anything nobler than a Ford and not even that till next year at the earliest ... None of these improvements has cost much. The stone for the cottage was dug out of our garden and the slates were bought two years ago for the Castle, which has to be concreted over instead, for our builder declares that no slate would withstand the storms. I went on my last American tour for Ballylee and that money is not all gone yet.

It is a great pleasure to live in a place where George makes at every moment a fourteenth century picture. And out of doors, with the hawthorn all in blossom all along the river banks, everything is so beautiful that to go elsewhere is to leave beauty behind.

– Letters, 1954

As for the name 'Thoor Ballylee', Yeats explained it in a letter to Olivia Shakespear in April 1922.

What do you think of our address – Thoor Ballylee? Thoor is Irish for tower and it will keep people from suspecting us of modern gothic and a

deer park. I think the harsh sound of 'Thoor' amends the softness of the rest.
  – Letters, 1954

Many of the poems in *The Tower* (1928) and *The Winding Stair* (1933) were written in, and inspired by, Yeats's new home. While planning how these books would look, Yeats instructed his friend, the artist Thomas Sturge Moore, to 'design the cover-design in gold and a frontispiece. The book is to be called *The Tower*, as a number of the poems were

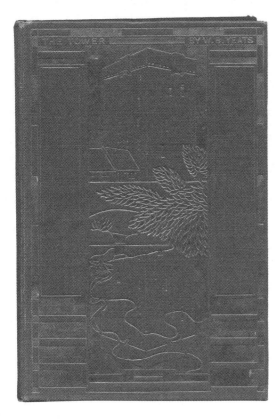

The Tower by W.B. Yeats

written at and about Ballylee Castle … It is a most impressive building and what I want is an imaginative impression. Do what you want with cloud and bird, day and night, but leave the great walls as they are' (*Letters*, 1954).

But life at Thoor Ballylee was not always tranquil. The Civil War of 1922–1923 had an impact throughout Ireland, and many scenes of hostility were experienced in the west. On August 19th, 1922, the conflict came perilously close to the Yeatses as they huddled on the winding stair of their tower while republican soldiers dynamited the bridge outside their home.

'The Stare's Nest by My Window'

The bees build in the crevices
Of loosening masonry, and there
The mother birds bring grubs and flies.
My wall is loosening; honey-bees,
Come build in the empty house of the stare.

We are closed in, and the key is turned
On our uncertainty; somewhere
A man is killed, or a house burned,
Yet no clear fact to be discerned:
Come build in the empty house of the stare.

A barricade of stone or of wood;
Some fourteen days of civil war;
Last night they trundled down the road
That dead young soldier in his blood:

Come build in the empty house of the stare.

We had fed the heart on fantasies,
The heart's grown brutal from the fare;
More substance in our enmities
Than in our love; O honey-bees,
Come build in the empty house of the stare.

– The Tower, 1928

In a letter to his friend John Quinn in 1918, Yeats had expressed his desire to make Thoor Ballylee 'a setting for my old age, a place to influence lawless youth, with its severity and antiquity' (*Letters*, 1954). However, as the years went on, increasing illnesses prevented him from travelling there, and on medical advice he and George began to spend their winters abroad and far from the damp and occasionally flooding tower they had deeply loved. After 1928 they did not return again and the tower fell into disrepair. It was eventually donated to the State by Yeats's son Michael, and through local efforts allied with national support, it was reopened as a museum on June 20th, 1965, to mark the centenary of Yeats's birth.

Now it is open to the public during the summer season, with some of the original furniture made from Irish elm on display. The river still chuckles, and the walk along it to the ruin of the old mill gives one some idea of the tranquillity that Yeats and his family knew at this place. On a wall of the tower is inscribed:

I, the poet William Yeats,
With old mill boards and sea-green slates,
And smithy work from the Gort forge,
Restored this tower for my wife George.
And may these characters remain
When all is ruin once again.

* * *

Yeats embraces much of the life and place of Co. Galway in his poem 'In Memory of Major Robert Gregory', written in 1918. He calls up images of Kiltartan, the townland in which Coole is located, Castle Taylor and Roxborough, Lady Gregory's ancestral home, as well as Esserkelly (Isserkelly) Plain and Mooneen (Moneen), north east of Gort, where Gregory rode with hounds. He was much affected by the death of his dear friend's son and the same year wrote another poem in Robert's memory, 'An Irish Airman Foresees His Death'. Both poems are from his collection *The Wild Swans at Coole* (1919).

'In Memory of Major Robert Gregory'

Now that we're almost settled in our house
I'll name the friends that cannot sup with us
Beside a fire of turf in th' ancient tower,
And having talked to some late hour
Climb up the narrow winding stair to bed:
Discoverers of forgotten truth
Or mere companions of my youth,
All, all are in my thoughts to-night being dead. ...

The Winding Stair by W.B. Yeats

When with the Galway foxhounds he would ride
From Castle Taylor to the Roxborough side
Or Esserkelly plain, few kept his pace;
At Mooneen he had leaped a place
So perilous that half the astonished meet
Had shut their eyes; and where was it
He rode a race without a bit?
And yet his mind outran the horses' feet.

We dreamed that a great painter had been born
To cold Clare rock and Galway rock and thorn,
To that stern colour and that delicate line
That are our secret discipline
Wherein the gazing heart doubles her might.
Soldier, scholar, horseman, he,
And yet he had the intensity
To have published all to be a world's delight.

* * *

'An Irish Airman Foresees his Death'

I know that I shall meet my fate
Somewhere among the clouds above;
Those that I fight I do not hate,
Those that I guard I do not love;
My country is Kiltartan Cross,
My countrymen Kiltartan's poor,
No likely end could bring them loss
Or leave them happier than before.

Nor law, nor duty bade me fight,

Nor public men, nor cheering crowds,

A lonely impulse of delight

Drove to this tumult in the clouds;

I balanced all, brought all to mind,

The years to come seemed waste of breath,

A waste of breath the years behind

In balance with this life, this death.

* * *

Yeats's first visit to Tulira Castle was with his friend Arthur Symons in summer 1896, during their hiking tour of the west of Ireland. Symons edited *Savoy* magazine, a London literary journal to which the eccentric owner of Tulira Castle, Edward Martyn, contributed. Martyn was to be a formative member of the triumvirate that laid the foundations for the Irish National Theatre, guaranteeing funding for the first three seasons. He was a devout Catholic and had ascetic tendencies, living an almost monastic existence in the tower he had added to the castle and in his cheap 'apartment' in Dublin, where he stayed in the poorer quarters above a shop without any obvious need for domestic attention. Of Martyn, Yeats said: 'He drank little, ate enormously, but thought himself an ascetic because he had but one meal a day, and suffered, though a courteous man, from a subconscious hatred of women' (*Dramatis Personae*, 1936).

Martyn's mischievous cousin was the writer George Moore, who spent a great deal of time at Tulira Castle.

They were cousins and inseparable friends, bound one to the other by mutual contempt. When I told Martyn that Moore had good points, he replied: 'I know Moore a great deal longer than you do. He has no good points.' And a week later Moore said: 'That man Martyn is the most selfish man alive. He thinks that I am damned and he doesn't care.'

– Dramatis Personae, 1936

Visiting Tulira Castle for the first time, Yeats wrote:

Edward Martyn brought us up the wide stairs of his Gothic Hall decorated by Crace and showed us our rooms. 'You can take your choice,' he said … Upon several evenings we asked Edward Martyn to extinguish all light except that of a little Roman lamp, sat there in the shadows, as though upon a stage set for Parsifal. Edward Martyn sat at his harmonium, so placed among the pillars that it seemed some ancient instrument, and played Palestrina.

George Moore

Yeats was initially fascinated by the architecture in its various manifestations of the medieval and Gothic styles of Tulira Castle, but later was less impressed.

Edward Martyn's clumsy body, where one already saw that likeness to a parish priest now so plain, the sign of his mother's peasant blood, had not suggested to me a house where, for all the bad Gothic of the modern part, there is spaciousness and state.

– Memoirs, 1972

During his first visit to Tulira Castle, Yeats evoked the power of the moon – which he saw as a powerful source of inspiration – then shared with Martyn details of his dreams, some of which were of an erotic nature. This angered Martyn, offending his Catholic sensibilities. Yeats had had those dreams in the room above the chapel in the old tower of the castle, which, according to Martyn, should remain empty, as any obstruction, such as the consequences of Yeats's invocations, might compromise 'the passage of prayer' (*Memoirs*, 1972).

Of the four great houses in this area to which Yeats and his close friends had connections, only Tulira Castle is still occupied. Roxborough was burned down during the Irish Civil War, while Castle Taylor and Coole Park are now in ruins.

Edward Martyn aspired to be a playwright, and his play *The Heather Field* premiered in May 1899 at the Antient Concert Rooms in Dublin, the day after Yeats's *The Countess Cathleen* opened as the Irish Literary Theatre's first production. The following year, during the ILT's second season, Martyn's play

Maeve was performed. Yeats and Lady Gregory saw him as a great prospect for their theatre, but Martyn had no desire to write plays about anything but the Irish peasantry. This and his purist Catholicism, in Yeats's opinion, held back Martyn's creative and intellectual development and ultimately caused a rift between them that ended Martyn's involvement in the Abbey Theatre and overshadowed their friendship.

* * *

Duras House on the shores of Kinvara Bay was the location for a metamorphic meeting between Yeats and Lady Gregory one wet afternoon in June 1896 that spawned the Irish Literary Theatre. The small two-storey house was built by the de Basterot family in 1810 and was, at the time of Yeats's visit with his friend Arthur Symons, owned by Florimond de Basterot, a French count and poet who played a benign supportive role in local literary circles.

He was a Catholic, an old man crippled by the sins of his youth, much devoted to his prayers, but an accomplished man of the world. He had flats in Paris and in Rome and divided his year between them and his little Galway house, passing through Dublin as quickly as possible because he thought it 'a shabby England'.
– *Dramatis Personae*, 1936

Recalling that 1896 gathering, Lady Gregory wrote:

We sat there through that wet afternoon, and though I had never been interested in theatres, our talk turned on plays … I said it was a pity we had no Irish theatre where such plays could be given. Mr. Yeats said that had always been a dream of his, but he had of late thought it an impossible one, for it could not at first pay its way, and there was no money to be found for such a thing in Ireland. We went on talking about it, and things seemed to grow possible as we talked, and before the end of the afternoon we had made our plan. We said we would collect money, or rather ask for a certain sum of money to be guaranteed. We would then take a Dublin theatre and give a performance of Mr. Martyn's 'Heather Field' and one of Mr. Yeats's own plays, 'The Countess Cathleen'. I offered the first guarantee of twenty-five pounds.

– Our Irish Theatre by Lady Gregory, 1913

Duras (Doorus) House was donated to An Óige, the Irish Youth Hostel Association, in 1961, and it still functions as a hostel. The Yeats connection is acknowledged by a plaque that records that historic meeting in 1896.

* * *

The man most important to the future was certainly Dr. Douglas Hyde. I had found a publisher while still in London for his 'Beside the Fire' and 'Love Songs of Connacht' and it was the first literary use of the English dialect of the Connacht country people that had roused my imagination for these books.

– Reveries, 1915

So said Yeats of Douglas Hyde, whom he had met at one of John O'Leary's gatherings in Rathmines when Hyde was still a student 'who took snuff like those Mayo country people, whose stories and songs he was writing down'.

Hyde was the son of a Church of Ireland minister and had spent his early years in Co. Sligo. The family moved to Frenchpark in Co. Roscommon in 1867 when Hyde's father was appointed rector there. Hyde was to become one of the earliest and most influential scholars of the Irish language and was greatly responsible for its revival and for the establishment of the Gaelic League (Conradh na Gaeilge) in 1893, of which he was the first president. Yeats recognised in Douglas Hyde both the talent and enthusiasm for reclaiming and celebrating the Irish language through its folk and fairytales.

His perpetual association with peasants, whose songs and stories he took down in their cottages from early childhood when he learned Irish from an old man on a kitchen floor, had given him, though a strong man, that cunning that is the strength of the weak. He was always diplomaticizing, evading as far as he could prominent positions and the familiarity of his fellows that he might escape jealousy and detraction.
  – *Memoirs*, 1972

If Hyde was trying to avoid prominent positions, he clearly did not succeed. Not only was he the first president of the Gaelic League, but in 1938 he was also appointed the first president of Ireland – possibly as a result of his 'diplomaticizing'. When Yeats first visited Hyde at his home at Frenchpark, Co. Roscommon, in April 1895, Hyde told him 'that I was the only man from Dublin who had ever stayed in his house' (*Memoirs*, 1972).

Douglas Hyde

During that visit Hyde and Yeats went to Lough Key near Boyle in Co. Roscommon. The visit aroused in Yeats images of a locus for his Celtic Mystical Order. Though it remained unrealised in the form that he originally envisioned, this idea remained with him until his final years, as we have seen when he reminded Maud Gonne of their dream of a 'Castle of Heroes' during their final meeting at Riversdale.

On a visit to Dr. Hyde I had seen the Castle Rock, as it was called in Lough Key. There is a small island entirely covered by what was a still habitable but empty castle … All round were the wooded and hilly shores, a place of great beauty. I believed that the castle could be hired for little money, and had long been dreaming of making it an Irish Eleusis or Samothrace. An obsession more constant than anything but my love itself was the need of mystical rites … to reunite the perception of the spirit, of the divine, with natural beauty … I was convinced that all lonely and lovely places were crowded with invisible beings and that it would be possible to communicate with them. I meant to initiate young men and women in this worship, which would unite the radical truths of Christianity to those of a more ancient world, and to use the Castle Rock for their occasional retirement from the world.
– Autobiographies, 1927

Though Yeats and Hyde admired each other's work and achievements, they each had reservations about the other's personality. Yeats thought Hyde was inclined to disguise his true feelings in company. And certainly during the early years of their friendship, Hyde claimed that 'he was bored to death with [Yeats's] blather', and that the poet had a tendency to try to dominate conversations and attract attention. Still, throughout their lives they supported each other, recognising a similar aspiration for a renaissance of Irish language, culture and folklore.

Castle Island in Lough Key Forest Park

LONDON

At length when I was eight or nine an aunt said to me,
'You are going to London. Here you are somebody.
There you will be nobody at all.'
– Reveries, 1915

Round Pond in Kensington Gardens

Kensington Gardens

I remember sitting upon somebody's knee, looking out of an Irish window at a wall covered with cracked and falling plaster, but what wall I do not remember, and being told that some relation once lived there. I am looking out of a window in London. It is in Fitzroy Road. Some boys are playing in the road and among them a boy in uniform, a telegraph-boy perhaps. When I ask who the boy is, a servant tells me that he is going to blow the town up, and I go to sleep in terror.

– *Reveries*, 1915

Much of W.B. Yeats's early childhood was spent in London. The poet's father, John Butler Yeats, believed that there he could establish himself as a sought-after portrait painter. Though he was called to the bar in 1866, by spring of 1867 he had given up the law – which had promised so much in terms of security – and moved to London to enroll at the Heatherley School of Fine Art to pursue a career as a painter. He was joined in July of that year by his wife Susan and their two children, Willie and Lily, and Isabella Pollexfen, Susan Yeats's eighteen-year-old sister, who acted as a nanny.

The family's first home in London was 23 Fitzroy Road, Primrose Hill, near Regent's Park. (Incidentally, this modest terraced house was also the place where the American poet Sylvia Plath took her own life in February 1963.)

JBY signed a six-year lease on the narrow three-storey home that began on July 1st, 1867, when Willie was just two years old. Three more Yeats children were born while the family lived at Fitzroy Road: Elizabeth Corbet ('Lolly', in 1868),

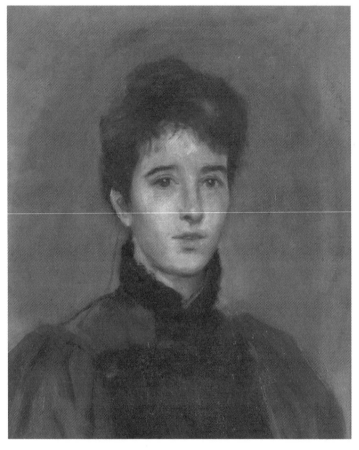

Elizabeth Corbet 'Lolly' Yeats by John Butler Yeats

Robert ('Bobbie', in 1870) and Jack (in 1871).

The family's stay here was punctuated by summers spent in Sligo. For the young Yeats children, Sligo was a paradise filled with horses, ships and the sea, and the adventures they read about in the books in the library at their grandparents' home, Merville. To their impressionable minds, it seemed that 'in Sligo the servants knew so intimately angels, saints, Banshees, and fairies. In London they talked of nothing but suicides and murders' (Lily Yeats's unpublished scrapbook).

In Sligo, they were also absorbed into the everyday lives of their uncles, aunts, cousins and servants; this contrasted greatly with the world they knew in London, where their father maintained a penurious situation as art student, father and absentee landlord from his low-yielding inherited properties at Thomastown, Co. Kilkenny. He seemed unable to finish anything off and was acutely aware of the expectations placed on him by his in-laws. His income as a landlord was exceeded by his expenditure, and to his great embarrassment and indignity, he had to borrow money from the Pollexfens, who did not fail to remind him that they hoped to see some return on their financial support in the form of his obtaining paid commissions.

Fitzroy Road served as both home and art studio, making it a cramped space in which to rear the children, and the young parents found life there oppressively hard. Susan Yeats in particular was unhappy in London, and she took every opportunity to return to Sligo, travelling via Liverpool on one of her father's ships. Most summers were spent in Ireland, and from 1872, the family remained in Sligo for over two years. It was during this stay that 'Bobbie' Yeats died suddenly of the croup, at age three.

In London, JBY moved from the Heatherley School of Fine Art to the Slade School of Art, where he took lessons under the renowned portrait painter Edward Poynter. However, though his intention was to do good work that would provide him with commercial success, by July 1873, at the expiration of the lease on Fitzroy Road, JBY returned to his family in Ireland. He began to receive commissions for portraits of the Herbert family, which took him to Muckross Abbey in Killarney, Co. Kerry. He was also commissioned to paint the Cosby children of Stradbally Hall, Co. Laois, which he completed during the winter and spring of 1873–1874.

In 1874, when W.B. Yeats was nine years old, with JBY still believing his career prospects lay in London, the Yeats family decided to move back from their extended stay in Sligo. They found a house at 14 Edith Villas, North End. Yeats found London a vast and lonely place. He was intensely homesick for Sligo and longed for some physical reminder of the place where he'd spent the previous two years. Later he was to write that he 'longed for a sod of earth from some field I knew, something of Sligo to hold in my hand' (*Reveries*, 1915).

The Yeats siblings were united in their loneliness. Willie and his sister Lily, a year younger, became very close, taking long walks together to the National Gallery and the Kensington Gardens pond, known as the Round Pond, where they would sail model boats. Yeats recalled those days in *Reveries*:

When my father gave me a holiday and later when I had a holiday from school I took my schooner boat to the Round Pond, sailing it very commonly against the two cutter yachts of an old naval officer. He would sometimes look at the ducks and say, 'I would like to take that fellow home for my dinner', and he sang me a sailor's song about a 'coffin ship' which left Sligo after the great famine, that made me feel very important.

Susan shared her children's homesickness and felt out of place in Edith Villas. While JBY had his artistic and literary friends, his stuttering career as a bohemian artist, and his studio in the cramped house, Susan herself was miserable. She felt excluded from her husband's world, though she did not profess any desire to be a part of it. The family also lived in constant debt. To further complicate matters, Susan became pregnant shortly after arriving in London, and Jane Grace was born in August 1875. Sadly, she died of bronchial pneumonia in June 1876, compounding Susan's unhappiness.

I can see now that she had great depth of feeling, that she was her father's daughter. My memory of what she was like in those days has grown very dim, but I think her sense of personality, her desire of any life of her own, had disappeared in her care for us and in much anxiety about money. I always see her sewing or knitting in spectacles and wearing some plain dress. Yet ten years ago when I was in San Francisco, an old

Burnham Beeches

cripple came to see me who had left Sligo before her marriage; he came to
tell me, he said, that my mother 'had been the most beautiful girl in Sligo'.
  – Autobiographies, 1927

In late autumn 1876, after spending another summer in
Sligo, JBY returned to England without his family to go to
Burnham Beeches (a nature reserve about twenty-five miles
west of Kensington) to study landscape painting. He sent for
Willie to join him. The eleven-year-old took great delight in
his freedom, fishing, collecting newts and shooting sparrows,
but Sligo was never far from his thoughts:

I did not know what it was to be alone, for I could wander in pleasant
alarm through the enclosed parts of the Beeches, then very large, or round
some pond imagining ships going in and out among the reeds and think-
ing of Sligo or of strange sea-faring adventures in the fine ship I should
launch when I grew up.
  – Reveries, 1915

Susan and the rest of the Yeats family returned from Sligo
to Edith Villas the following year, and Yeats was enrolled at
Godolphin School in Iffley Road, Hammersmith, where he
would study for five years.

The only lessons I had ever learned were those my father taught me, for
he terrified me by descriptions of my moral degradation and he humili-
ated me by my likeness to disagreeable people; but presently I was sent to
school in Hammersmith. It was a Gothic building of yellow brick: a large
hall full of desks, some small classrooms, and a separate house for boarders,
all built perhaps in 1860 or 1870. I thought it an ancient building and

that it had belonged to the founder of the school, Lord Godolphin, who was romantic to me because there was a novel about him. On one side there was a piano factory of yellow brick, upon two sides half-finished rows of little shops and villas all yellow brick, and on the fourth side, outside the wall of our playing field, a brick field of cinders and piles of half-burned yellow bricks.

– Reveries, 1915

Yeats found the other pupils overly concerned about his father's status and income, values remote from those of his own bohemian household. He also found himself fighting with the other boys.

... I was called names for being Irish, and had many fights and never, for years, got the better in any one of them; for I was delicate and had no muscles.

– Reveries, 1915

He became increasingly aware of his Irishness and had a sense of not fitting in with the other boys at Godolphin. At times he almost seemed to provoke them into attacking him.

There was a boy with a big stride, much feared by little boys, and find-ing him alone in the playing-field, I went up to him and said, 'Rise upon Sugaun and sink upon Gad'. 'What does that mean?' he said. 'Rise upon hay-leg and sink upon straw', I answered, and told him that in Ireland the sergeant tied straw and hay to the ankles of a stupid recruit to show him the difference between his legs. My ears were boxed, and when I complained to my friends, they said I had brought it upon myself; and that I deserved all I got.

The Godolphin School in Hammersmith

Yeats's heart and soul remained in Ireland, and he held his own prejudicial feelings towards the English, no doubt inspired by the strongly held opinions of his relatives. Those family members in Sligo may have 'despised Nationalists and Catholics, but all disliked England with a prejudice that had come perhaps from the days of the Irish Parliament. I knew stories to the discredit of England, and took them all seriously' (*Reveries*, 1915).

Susan Yeats herself was not above disseminating prejudice in her son's attitude towards the English.

My mother had shown them to me kissing at railway stations, and taught me to feel disgust at their lack of reserve, and my father told how my grandfather, William Yeats ... spoke of some man he had met on a coach road who 'Englishman-like' told him all his affairs.

– *Reveries*, 1915

Life was emotionally and physically hard for the sensitive young Yeats. Fear haunted him, not just of his father but of the other boys and teachers, influencing his own sense of honour and self-worth.

I was very much afraid of physical pain, and one day when I had made some noise in class, my friend the athlete was accused and I allowed him to get two strokes of the cane before I gave myself up. He had held out his hands without flinching and had not rubbed them on his sides afterwards. I was not caned, but was made to stand up for the rest of the lesson. I suffered very much afterwards when the thought came to me, but he did not reproach me.
– Reveries, 1915

Constant bullying at the Godolphin School prompted Yeats to take boxing lessons from an athlete friend, who refused to protect him any longer. When another boy called him a 'Mad Irishman', Yeats 'hit him several times on the face without being hit, till the boys round said we should make friends. I held out my hand in fear, for I knew if we went on I should be beaten, and he took it sullenly. I had so poor a reputation as a fighter that it was a great disgrace to him, and even the masters made fun of his swollen face ... I never had another fight with a school-fellow' (*Reveries*, 1915).

Academically Yeats was very much below average. His half-yearly report for Lent Term 1877 showed him to be twenty-first overall of thirty-one boys in the class, being sixth in classics, twenty-seventh in mathematics, eighteenth in modern languages, and nineteenth in English with the comment 'Very poor in spelling' in the report's additional notes. (His class-mate from High School Dublin – where Yeats was enrolled from 1881 onwards – would report that he was strong in mathematics, indicating that he later made improvements in at least one subject.) His father was not impressed by the English education system, which he felt did not necessarily recognise the need to learn 'to believe in art and poetry and the sovereignty of intellect and of the spirit' that he strived to inculcate in Willie's mind through his home-schooling.

In his later years, Yeats would describe the Godolphin School as 'an obscene, bullying place, where a big boy would hit a small boy in the wind to see him double up, and where certain boys, too young for any emotion of sex, would sing the dirty songs of the street, but I daresay it suited me better than a better school … I was unfitted for school work, and though I would often work well for weeks together, I had to give the whole evening to one lesson if I was to know it' (*Reveries*, 1915).

The Yeatses lived at England's first 'garden suburb', Bedford Park, from the spring of 1879, when Yeats was thirteen years old, until Autumn 1881, at which point the family moved back to Ireland. (They would move to Bedford Park again in 1887, after which Yeats began his itinerant lifestyle, moving back and forth between Ireland and England.)

Bedford Park was an attempt to create a self-sufficient com-munity of artists and art lovers in well-built spacious homes in the west of London, with an artistic ethos influencing the design and layout of the homes and the community buildings. It included a clubhouse with a theatre, small shops, a public house called The Tabard – named after the tavern in Chaucer's *Canterbury Tales* – a church, an athletic club and almost five hundred houses. Its plan incorporated the large old trees that stood on the estate.

After the cramped conditions at Edith Villas, Bedford Park seemed like a new world to the Yeatses.

We were to see De Morgan tiles, peacock-blue doors and the pomegranate pattern and the tulip pattern of Morris, and to discover that we had always hated doors painted with imitation grain, the roses of mid-Victoria, and tiles covered with geometrical patterns that seemed to have been shaken out of a muddy kaleidoscope. We went to live in a house like those we had seen in pictures and even met people dressed like people in the story books.

– Reveries, 1915

Nor was Yeats's childhood connection to the sea disappointed. Describing the Bedford Park house of the artist Thomas Matthews Rooke:

My two sisters and my brother and myself had dancing lessons in a low, red-brick and tiled house that drove away dreams, long cherished, of some day living in a house made exactly like a ship's cabin. The dining-room table, where Sinbad the sailor might have sat, was painted peacock-blue, and the woodwork was all peacock-blue and upstairs a window niche was so big and high up that there was a flight of steps to go up and down by and a table in the niche.

Though the family's living conditions had improved substantially, their financial situation had not. JBY could not manage to bring in a sufficient income, and it wasn't long before he was again sending for money from the Thomastown lands to subsidise their living expenses. The family's perilous financial situation meant that JBY was already thinking of ways to escape his lease at 8 Woodstock Road, Bedford Park, within a year of taking up residence there. By the autumn of 1881, and to Susan Yeats's delight, the family had decided to return to Ireland, where JBY would find a studio in Dublin. This move took them to Balscadden Cottage in Howth, north of Dublin.

* * *

In 1887 the Yeats family once again crossed the Irish Sea to London. This was the beginning of a significantly influential period in young Yeats's life. The following years would form the man and the poet in remarkable ways. He would discover his love for the theatre and his belief that a country deserved and was entitled to its own theatrical tradition. He would discover a community of like-minded poets, writers, painters and philosophers with whom he would remain in contact for the rest of his life. He would meet actors with whom he would forge long-lasting relationships, and he would be engulfed by the flames of an enduring passion that would inspire his writings until his death.

Already in London preparing for his family's arrival, JBY

The Yeats home at Blenheim Road, Bedford Park

had managed to find a small and undistinguished house at 58 Eardley Crescent near Earl's Court, where the family moved in May 1887. With them was their servant Rose and their black cat, named after the Great Liberator, Daniel O'Connell. Lily Yeats, in her unpublished scrapbook, described the house as being 'old and dirty, dark and noisy', though its proximity to the Earl's Court Arena was particularly exciting for young Jack B. Yeats, as the residents were given tickets to attend Buffalo Bill's extravaganza with horses, guns and native American Indians charging around. He was enthralled by the excitement and action, and his work almost always bore the hallmark of his innocent infatuation with movement and colour, and, quite frequently, with horses.

Willie, who had briefly lodged at 6 Berkley Road, Regent's Park, before joining the rest of the family when their new home was ready, had, at the age of twenty-one, already privately published a book, *Mosada,* and numerous poems in journals that had been well received, and he was considered a rising star of the literary scene. He began to write reviews and articles on folklore for mainly American newspapers that formed the basis of his book *The Celtic Twilight.* Still he chose to remain with his family and assumed a great deal of the financial responsibility.

It was in Eardley Crescent on August 11th, 1887, that Susan Yeats suffered the first of numerous strokes that were to cause her to become an invalid until her death in 1900. After her stroke, she and Lily went to stay with Susan's sister Elizabeth Pollexfen Orr in Denby near Huddersfield, Yorkshire, to recuperate, but while there she suffered a second stroke and fell down the stairs. The family concluded that the cramped and dingy conditions of the house at Eardley Crescent may have contributed in some way towards Susan's ill health, and they set about finding a more suitable home.

Their search brought them back to the spacious houses and tree-lined streets of Bedford Park. In March 1888, Yeats wrote to his friend Katharine Tynan,

We go to our new house, 3 Blenheim Road, Bedford Park, on the 25th of this month; a fine roomy house, which by good luck we have got very cheap. Bedford Park is the least Londonish place hereabouts, a silent tree-filled place where everything is a little idyllic, except the cockroaches which abound there.

– Letters, 1954

So it was that the Yeatses returned to Bedford Park. Susan and Lily rejoined them from Yorkshire. Yeats's past enthusiasm for the community had become somewhat tempered by the changes he witnessed.

Years before we had lived there, when the crooked ostentatiously picturesque streets with great trees casting great shadows had been a new enthusiasm: the Pre-Raphaelite movement at last affecting life. But now exaggerated criticism had taken the place of enthusiasm, the tiled roofs, the first in modern London, were said to leak, which they did not, and the drains to be bad, though that was no longer true: and I imagine that houses were cheap.

– Autobiographies, 1927

3 Blenheim Road became a gathering place for many of the influential players in the world of Victorian arts. Initially through JBY, but later through Yeats's own connections, writers, artists, actors and politicians came to visit or stay, filling the Yeats world with the excitement and eclecticism it craved and enjoyed. John O'Leary came; so too did Katharine Tynan, Douglas Hyde, T.W. Rolleston, the American poet Louise Imogen Guiney and many others. Significantly, it was at Bedford Park that Yeats first experienced drama made flesh in the form of John Todhunter's poetic drama *A Sicilian Idyll*, which was performed at the clubhouse in May 1890, with the professional actress Florence Farr in a leading role. In his review of the play published in *The Boston Pilot* (1890), Yeats wrote of 'her striking beauty and subtle gesture and fine delivery of the verse'. He later collaborated with Farr on many theatrical projects including her directing of and acting in the Irish Literary Theatre's debut play *The Countess Cathleen* at the Antient Concert Rooms in Dublin in May 1899.

Katharine Tynan, in *Reminiscences* (1913) recounts visiting Yeats at Blenheim Road in 1893:

His study is at the back of a quaint and charming house, in which, outside the poet's den, order reigns. It opens on a little balcony, twined about and overhung with Virginia creeper. He has generally a few plants there of which he is inordinately jealous. Indeed, one of the few occasions on which I have seen his placid temper roused was when some teasing person pretended to annex the faint blossoms he had coaxed into existence. In the study confusion reigns paramount. The fireplace, which makes a slanting projection, is littered with papers. The mantelpiece is buried in layers of

Self-portrait by John Butler Yeats

them. Books are everywhere – on shelves, chairs, table, and mantelpiece. When the poet wishes to invite your attention to any particular book or paper, he sweeps the dusky hair with his hand from his beautiful forehead – a gesture telling of effort and endeavor. On the ceiling he has painted a map of Sligo, with a ship at each corner.

Most significantly, a meeting was to take place at 3 Blenheim Road that would profoundly influence the very essence of Yeats's personal, literary and political life.

I was twenty-three years old when the troubling of my life began. I had heard from time to time in letters from Miss [Ellen] O'Leary, John O'Leary's old sister, of a beautiful girl who had left the society of the Vice-regal Court for Dublin nationalism. In after years I persuaded myself that I felt premonitory excitement at the first reading of her name. Presently she drove up to our house in Bedford Park with an introduction from John O'Leary to my father. I had never thought to see in a living woman so great beauty. It belonged to famous pictures, to poetry, to some legendary past. A complexion like the blossom of apples, and yet face and body had the beauty of lineaments which Blake calls the highest beauty because it changes least from youth to age, and a stature so great that she seemed of a divine race.

– Autobiographies, 1927

Thus Yeats described his first encounter with Maud Gonne on January 30th, 1889; the woman who would consume much of his being for the rest of his life, and who would fill his verse and his days with joy and sorrow, admiration and admonition, inspiration and disappointment, but always respect and love.

'Pilgrim soul': Maud Gonne

Gonne, a year younger than Yeats, was born in England, the daughter of an officer in the British Army who was posted to the Curragh in Co. Kildare when Maud was two years old. Three years later, her mother died of tuberculosis, and the family moved to Dublin, followed by the Hill of Howth, where they remained until 1874, some years before the Yeats family moved there. Yeats idolised Gonne from the moment they first met, and he made no attempt to conceal his love for her.

'The Arrow'

I thought of your beauty, and this arrow,
Made out of a wild thought, is in my marrow.
There's no man may look upon her, no man,
As when newly grown to be a woman,
Tall and noble but with face and bosom
Delicate in colour as apple blossom.
This beauty's kinder, yet for a reason
I could weep that the old is out of season.

– In the Seven Woods, 1904

For much of his life Yeats sought to marry her, proposing to her on numerous occasions, the first time in Dublin in August 1891.

I asked her to marry me. I remember a curious thing. I had come into the room with that purpose in mind, and hardly looked at her or thought of her beauty. At once I knew that my confidence had gone, and an instant later she drew her hand away. No, she could not marry – there were reasons – She would never marry; but in words that had no conventional ring she asked for my friendship.
  – Autobiographies, 1927

Yeats and Gonne spent the next day on Howth Head as described elsewhere in this book. At that time Yeats wrote one of his best-known poems about Gonne:

'When You are Old'

When you are old and grey and full of sleep,
And nodding by the fire, take down this book,
And slowly read, and dream of the soft look
Your eyes had once, and of their shadows deep;

How many loved your moments of glad grace,
And loved your beauty with love false or true,
But one man loved the pilgrim soul in you,
And loved the sorrows of your changing face;

And bending down beside the glowing bars,
Murmur, a little sadly, how Love fled
And paced upon the mountains overhead
And hid his face amid a crowd of stars.

– Poems, 1895

Unfortunately for Yeats, Gonne repeatedly made it clear that she did not consider marriage, or even a romantic affair, a possibility, and for her own reasons, she concealed the fact that she was already in a relationship with the French journalist and politician Lucien Millevoye. She would go on to conceal the fact that she had two children with Millevoye, one of whom, Georges Silvère, died of meningitis as an infant.

It was not only Gonne's appearance that captivated Yeats. Her political activism, particularly on behalf of Irish independence, instilled in him both a sense of awe and despair. During the course of her life she either founded or was involved with the Gaelic League, the Land League, Inghinidhe na hÉireann (Daughters of Ireland) and the Women's Prisoners' Defence

League, and other movements to which she committed her-
self unconditionally.

*Every speech has been a triumph, and every triumph greater than the
one that went before it. Thousands who come to see this new wonder – a
beautiful woman who makes speeches – remain to listen with delight to
her sincere and simple eloquence.*
– *The Boston Pilot*, 1892

At times Yeats approved of Maud's activism; at other times
he found it counter-productive at the political level, particu-
larly when he became a senator and they found themselves at
opposite ends of the political spectrum. They had fallings-out
too, but never to the extent that they were unable to reconcile
their differences, and Yeats continued to support and assist
Gonne throughout his life.

Yeats's confusion about the impact of Gonne on his life and
on the political unrest of Victorian Ireland is expressed in 'No
Second Troy'.

Why should I blame her that she filled my days
With misery, or that she would of late
Have taught to ignorant men most violent ways,
Or hurled the little streets upon the great,
Had they but courage equal to desire?
What could have made her peaceful with a mind
That nobleness made simple as a fire,
With beauty like a tightened bow, a kind

That is not natural in an age like this,
Being high and solitary and most stern?
Why, what could she have done, being what she is?
Was there another Troy for her to burn?

– *The Green Helmet*, 1910

After separating from Lucien Millevoye, Maud married Irish republican and military leader John MacBride, with whom she had a son, Sean. The couple were estranged by the time MacBride was executed, in May 1916, for his part in the Easter Rising. The following month, Yeats travelled to Normandy, France, to stay with the Gonnes, and for the final time, he asked Maud to marry him. When he declared that he was not able to live without her and that he was miserable, she replied: 'Oh yes, you are, because you make beautiful poetry out of what you call your unhappiness and are happy in that. Marriage would be such a dull affair. Poets should never marry. The world should thank me for not marrying you' (*A Servant of the Queen* by Maud Gonne, 1950).

In August 1916, while still in Normandy, he turned his attentions to Maud's daughter, Iseult, and proposed to her. She also declined. The next year he returned to Normandy and in August proposed once again to Iseult, who again refused him. Finally, after travelling back to England with Maud and Iseult, with whom he discussed his intention to ask George Hyde-Lees to marry him, he proposed to and married George all within a few weeks in the autumn of 1917, when she was twenty-five years of age and Yeats was fifty-two.

Yeats said that George enabled him to access real wisdom

W.B. and George Yeats with their two children, Anne and Michael

and knowledge by means of her ability to act as a cipher for the occupants of the spiritual world through 'automatic writing', which allowed the 'spirits' to use her hand as their own. Their work together in this regard produced the book *A Vision* in 1925, which is based on a series of automatic writings that trace the passage of the soul through the various phases of the moon. The couple had two children, Anne (1919–2001) and Michael (1921–2007). Anne would grow up to be a painter and stage designer; Michael, a barrister and senator.

After Yeats and George married, his relationship with Maud Gonne waned, though their names and lives had by that time become inseparably bound. Gonne became less involved in Irish politics; her son, Sean MacBride, would become a cabinet minister in the Irish government.

If any man grew near
When I was young,
I thought, 'He holds her dear,'
And shook with hate and fear.
But O! 'twas bitter wrong
If he could pass her by
With an indifferent eye.
Whereon I wrote and wrought,
And now, being grey,
I dream that I have brought
To such a pitch my thought
That coming time can say,
'He shadowed in a glass
What thing her body was.'
For she had fiery blood
When I was young,
And trod so sweetly proud
As 'twere upon a cloud,
A woman Homer sung,
That life and letters seem
But an heroic dream.

– from 'A Woman Homer Sung' (*The Green Helmet*, 1910)

* * *

In October 1895 and at the age of thirty, Yeats finally left home permanently. His parents and siblings continued to live at Bedford Park, but Yeats struck out for independence, sharing rooms with his friend Arthur Symons at 2 Fountain Court, Middle Temple.

Hitherto when in London I had stayed with my family in Bedford Park, but now I was to live for some twelve months [it was actually six months] in chambers in the temple that opened through a little passage into those of Arthur Symons. If anybody rang at either door, one or other would look through a window in the connecting passage, and report. We would then decide whether one or both should receive the visitor, whether his door or mine should be opened, or whether both doors were to remain closed.

– The Trembling of the Veil, 1922

Symons had become Yeats's dear and close friend and confidant during this period of emotional turmoil with his all-consuming love for Maud Gonne pre-eminent.

He had the sympathetic intelligence of a woman, and was the best listener I have ever met … Symons more than any man I have ever known, could slip as it were into the mind of another, and my thoughts gained in richness and in clearness from his sympathy.

– Autobiographies, 1927

In February 1896, Yeats moved to 18 Woburn Buildings (now 5 Woburn Walk) near St. Pancras Station. In his grief over his failed pursuit of Maud Gonne, he had begun a relationship with Olivia Shakespear, a married woman introduced to him by her cousin Lionel Johnson. Yeats named Shakespear 'Diana Vernon' in his memoirs to conceal her true identity. His

The poet pictured at home in 18 Woburn Buildings

desire to consummate their furtive relationship accelerated his departure from Fountain Court into the quiet, shoddy streets of the northern end of Bloomsbury, where Yeats took a lease on two floors of a terraced house.

I took my present rooms at Woburn Buildings and furnished them very meagerly with such cheap furniture as I could throw away without regret as I grew more prosperous. She came with me to make every purchase, and I remember an embarrassed conversation in the presence of some Tottenham Court [Road] shop man upon the width of the bed – every inch increased the expense.

– Dramatis Personae, 1936

'Diana Vernon': W.B. Yeats's lover Olivia Shakespear

Their relationship as lovers was fraught with difficulties, socially, spiritually and physically, and it petered out a year later, hastened by Olivia's creeping suspicion that Yeats's heart lay elsewhere.

'There is someone else in your heart,' she said. It was the breaking between us for many years.
– *Autobiographies*, 1927

'The Lover Mourns for the Loss of Love'

Pale brows, still hands and dim hair,
I had a beautiful friend
And dreamed that the old despair
Would end in love in the end:
She looked in my heart one day
And saw your image was there;
She has gone weeping away.

– *The Wind Among the Reeds*, 1899

Ironically, Yeats would eventually marry Olivia's step-niece and her daughter Dorothy's best friend, George Hyde-Lees.

During the following twenty years, Yeats gradually acquired the rest of the building, taking over the attic, the first floor and then the ground floor. Woburn Buildings, like Bedford Park, became a centre for the burgeoning literary and artistic community that surrounded Yeats, and he established regular Monday evening 'soirées' at which writers and artists would

The Reading Room at the British Museum, drawn by C. Gregory

exchange ideas and discuss their work. Yeats remained at Woburn Buildings until June 1919, some two years after his marriage to George Hyde-Lees, when he gave up the lease.

* * *

I spent my days at the British Museum and must, I think, have been delicate, for I remember often putting off hour after hour consulting some necessary book because I shrank from lifting the heavy volumes of the catalogue; and yet to save money for my afternoon coffee and roll I often walked the whole way home to Bedford Park.

– Four Years, 1921

During the late 1880s and early 1890s Yeats visited the reading room at the British Museum library a great deal. There he found the space and quiet to write. He was busy in those days, not only working on his own poetry and plays but also writing to earn money to pour into the 'swalley hole', the term the Yeatses gave to the fund that supported the household. He contributed to newspapers and journals as diverse as *The Tract Society*, *The Girl's Own Paper*, *The Manchester Courier*, *The Leisure Hour* and *The Scots Observer*.

The statues that surrounded the library's reading room, with their evocation of mythical heroes, Greek athletes and Egyptian kings, became to the young Yeats 'images of an unpremeditated joyous energy, that neither I nor any other man, racked by doubt and inquiry, can achieve; and that yet, if once achieved, might seem to men and women of Connemara or of Galway their very soul' (*Four Years*, 1921).

Yeats's walks to and from the museum also inspired perhaps his best-known poem, as he described in *Reveries*:

> I was going along the Strand and, passing a shop window where there was a little ball kept dancing by a jet of water, I remembered waters about Sligo and was moved to a sudden emotion that shaped itself into 'The Lake Isle of Innisfree'.
> – *Reveries*, 1915

Over the course of time, Yeats began to recognise faces at the museum; many of these people would become close friends and influence his social, literary and spiritual development, such as Liddell Mathers.

At the British Museum Reading-Room I often saw a man of thirty-six, or thirty-seven, in a brown velveteen coat, with a gaunt resolute face, and an athletic body, who seemed, before I heard his name, or knew the nature of his studies, a figure of romance. Presently I was introduced, where or by what man or woman I do not remember. He was called Liddell Mathers, but would soon, under the touch of 'The Celtic Movement' become MacGregor Mathers, and then plain MacGregor. He was the author of 'The Kabbal Unveiled' and his studies were two only – magic and the theory of war.

– Four Years, 1921

Mathers introduced Yeats to the Hermetic Order of the Golden Dawn (also known as 'The Hermetic Students'), which Mathers had co-founded and into which Yeats was initiated in 1887 at a studio in Charlotte Street. Yeats had already been involved with the setting up of the Dublin Hermetic Society in 1885. He would spend the remainder of his life advancing through the order's hierarchy until he attained the rank of Imperator of the Temple of the Golden Dawn. Yeats's devotion to and belief in magic, the occult, astrology, alchemy, geomancy and the Kabbalah fired a spiritual flame throughout his life, and between them he found a form of religion that appeased his curious and unorthodox spirit. Mathers also hosted 'gatherings' at his home at Stent Lodge, Forest Hill, now part of the Horniman Museum. (Annie Horniman, heiress to a fortune accumulated through the tea trade, gave her financial support to the founding of the Irish National Theatre.)

Yeats had already met William Morris, who was, among

Kelmscott House, home of William Morris

other things, an artist, poet, novelist, philosopher, socialist and designer, at the Contemporary Club in Dublin in April 1886. He now began to attend gatherings at Morris's home, Kelmscott House, which backed onto the Thames in Hammersmith. Yeats discusses his association with Morris and his family and friends in *Reveries*:

> *I cannot remember who first brought me to the old stable beside Kelmscott House, William Morris's house at Hammersmith, and to the debates held there upon Sunday evenings by the Socialist League [of which Morris was a founding member]. I was soon of the little group who had supper with Morris afterwards. I met at these suppers very constantly Walter Crane, Emery Walker, in association with Cobden Sanderson, the printer of many fine books, and less constantly Bernard Shaw and Cockerell, now of the Museum of Cambridge, and perhaps but once or twice Hyndman the Socialist and the Anarchist Prince Kropotkin.*

As a child, Yeats had annoyed his father by seeming to prefer the writings of Morris to those of John Keats, his father's own favourite. As an adult, Yeats wrote that Morris's prose romances became 'the only books I was ever to read slowly that I might not come too quickly to the end'.

Though Yeats acclaimed Morris the novelist, he did not feel the same of Morris the poet. However, this did not prevent Yeats saying that 'if some angel offered me the choice, I would choose to live his life, poetry and all, rather than my own or any other man's'.

Yeats maintained his immense admiration for Morris throughout his life and, on the wall of his study at Riversdale,

Designs by William Morris

Rathfarnham, his final Irish home, hung a portrait of Morris.

If William Morris was to have a profound influence on W.B. Yeats, Morris's daughter Mary 'May' Morris was to have the same effect on his sisters, Lily and Lolly. May was a highly skilled embroiderer and designer, specialising in the exquisite free-formed embroidery that her father promoted in his designs. Willie and the girls took French lessons at Kelmscott House, where they met May. She asked Lily if she would like to learn embroidery and help her with her business, which Lily did, starting at ten shillings per week, enabling her to contribute in no small way to the Yeats family finances. May was bad-tempered and a taskmaster, and Lily found the work physically demanding, but she remained at Morris & Co. for six years, during which time she became an accomplished embroiderer. Meanwhile, Lolly attended art school and began teaching around the city. She also published three art books and made a good income from their sales.

On January 3rd, 1900, Susan Yeats died, ending her many years of suffering. She is buried at Acton Rural Cemetery, now Acton Cemetery, in the London Borough of Ealing. Susan's death allowed the family to consider other options regarding jobs and places to live, and in 1902, embroidery artist Evelyn Gleeson invited the Yeats sisters to Ireland to join with her in a business venture that sought to provide training and work for young Irish women in the skills of printing, weaving, embroidery and bookbinding. They set up in a large house in Dundrum, Dublin, named Runnymede, which they changed to Dun Emer. It was an idealistic venture, founded on a less than firm business footing; however, with the help of

Elizabeth Corbet 'Lolly' Yeats printing at Dun Emer, 1903

Willie and Jack, they slowly established themselves and began to create limited editions of books, broadsheets, carpets and other crafts in the spirit of the Arts and Crafts movement.

On their return from London JBY, Lily, Lolly, a cousin named Ruth, and two house-servants moved into a small house on Lower Churchtown Road named Gurteen Dhas ('pretty little field'). The house was located a few miles from Dun Emer; the sisters made the journey on foot four times each day, as they also returned home for lunch. Gurteen Dhas assumed the same role as Blenheim Road in London had done insofar as it became a gathering place for Dublin's artistic community. The actor/producer Willie Fay wrote: 'There was always a welcome for us, and over a cup or two, or maybe three, of coffee a fresh debate would start, the last play would be criticized or the prospects of the next one discussed. All the time our host would be busy in a corner with his sketch book, rapidly pencilling one of those delightful portraits that he was always creating whenever he had the chance' (*The Fays of the Abbey Theatre* by W.G. Fay & Catherine Carswell, 1935).

In 1908 the Yeats sisters parted from Gleeson and established Cuala Industries and the Cuala Press in neighbouring Churchtown. The emphasis was on new works by Irish writers, and over its lifetime it printed over seventy titles, of which almost fifty were by W.B. Yeats. Jack did many of the illustrations and artwork for the books, broadsheets, posters and other publications.

* * *

Throughout the 1890s and early 1900s, W.B. Yeats was energetically following his social, spiritual and literary trajectories. He maintained his interest in theosophy that had been kindled in Dublin in 1885. In May 1887 he visited Madame Helena Blavatsky, the 'high-priestess' of the Theosophical Society who had relocated to London to avoid legal complications resulting from an investigation by the Society of Psychical Research into her practices, which suggested charlatanism. Simply put, she believed that she was the cipher of two Tibetan 'mahatmas', Koot-Hoomi and Morya, and was chosen to transmit their message to the world. Yeats's first awkward and hilarious encounter with Madame Blavatsky at a small house called Maycot in Crownhill, Upper Norwood, is described in *Reveries*:

The Society of Psychical Research had just reported on her Indian phenomena – and as one of the three [remaining] followers sat in an outer room to keep out undesirable visitors, I was kept a long time kicking my heels. Presently I was admitted and found an old woman in a plain loose dark dress: a sort of Irish peasant woman with an air of humour and audacious power. I was still kept waiting, for she was deep in conversation with a woman visitor. I strayed through folding doors into the next room and stood, in sheer idleness of mind, looking at a cuckoo clock. It was certainly stopped, for the weights were off and lying upon the ground, and yet, as I stood there the cuckoo came out and cuckooed at me. I interrupted Madame Blavatsky to say, 'Your clock has hooted me.' 'It often hoots at a stranger,' she replied. 'Is there a spirit in it?' I said. 'I do not know,' she said, 'I should have to be alone to know what is in it.'

In 1888 he joined the Esoteric Section of the Theosophical Society, whose meetings took place at 17 Lansdowne Road, Holland Park. He hoped for opportunities to explore the mystical and magical aspects of the society's teachings. However, Madame Blavatsky was reluctant to encourage him in this, though he did experiment with trying to call forth the ghost of a flower back to life and trying to evoke specific dreams by sleeping with certain symbols in the bed. His 'maverick' spirit

Madame Helena Blavatsky

and refusal to follow instructions led Madame Blavatsky to expel him from the society, as he was 'causing discussion and disturbance' and was publicly critical of its work.

* * *

In England the writers do not form groups, but each man works by himself and for himself, for England is the land of literary Ishmaels. It is only among the sociable Celtic nations that men draw near to each other when they want to think and dream and work.

– 'The Rhymers' Club', published in *The Boston Pilot*. Quoted in *Letters to the New Island*, 1989

In January 1890 Yeats and Welsh writer Ernest Rhys formed The Rhymers' Club, whose meetings took place at the rambling Ye Olde Cheshire Cheese pub in Wine Office Court. The Cheshire Cheese had a long-established literary association already, Oliver Goldsmith having written much of *The Vicar of Wakefield* there. The meetings consisted of weekly gatherings for food in the downstairs section of the pub, followed by smoking, drinking and reading their work upstairs, subjecting it to discussion and criticism. Ernest Rhys was of the opinion that every man had a lyric or a piece of verse in his pocket, and the Rhymers' Club provided them with the opportunity to make it known. Regular attendees were Ernest Dowson, Edwin Ellis, Lionel Johnson, John Davidson, Richard Le Gallienne, T.W. Rolleston, John Todhunter and Arthur Symons. Sometimes, and only when the meetings were held at a member's house, Oscar Wilde attended; he considering the Cheshire Cheese too 'bohemian' for his liking. In *Four Years*, Yeats describes the often crowded gatherings at Ye Olde Cheshire Cheese.

I remember saying one night at the Cheshire Cheese, when more poets than usual had come, 'None of us can say who will succeed, or even who has or has not talent. The only thing certain about us is that we are too many.'

Yeats was told by a member years later that when he talked 'a gloomy silence fell upon the room' as he came across more as a man of letters than as a poet.

I wore a brown velveteen coat, a loose tie, and a very old Inverness cape, discarded by my father twenty years before and preserved by my Sligo-born mother whose actions were unreasoning and habitual like the seasons.

– *Four Years*, 1921

In 1892 the Rhymers' Club published the first of two anthologies, *The Book of the Rhymers' Club*. The book consisted of contributions from its members and included Yeats's poems 'The Man Who Dreamed of Faeryland', 'The Ballad of Father Gilligan', 'A Faery Song' and 'The Lake Isle of Innisfree'.

The Second Book of the Rhymers' Club followed in 1894, which included 'The Folk of the Air', 'The Fiddler of Dooney' and 'The Rose in My Heart' (later 'The Lover Tells of the Rose in His Heart').

'The Rose in My Heart'

All things uncomely and broken, all things worn out and old,
The cry of a child by the roadway, the creak of a lumbering cart,
The heavy steps of the ploughman, splashing the wintry mould,
Are wronging your image that blossoms a rose in the deeps of my heart.

The wrong of unshapely things is a wrong too great to be told;
I hunger to build them anew and sit on a green knoll apart,
With the earth and the sky and the water, re-made, like a casket of gold
For my dreams of your image that blossoms a rose in the deeps of
my heart.

The Rhymers' Club survived until 1894 and disbanded for a variety of reasons, including problems caused by drink or love affairs that went wrong, or suicide. Yeats pays homage to his fellow Cheshire Cheese poets and talks of their demise:

Since, tavern comrades, you have died,
Maybe your images have stood,
Mere bone and muscle thrown aside,
Before that roomful or as good.
You had to face your ends when young –
'Twas wine or women, or some curse –
But never made a poorer song
That you might have a heavier purse,
Nor gave loud service to a cause
That you might have a troop of friends,
You kept the Muses' sterner laws,
And unrepenting faced your ends,

> *And therefore earned the right – and yet*
> *Dowson and Johnson most I praise –*
> *To troop with those the world's forgot,*
> *And copy their proud steady gaze.*

– from 'The Grey Rock' *(Responsibilities,* 1914*)*

Yeats's hopes and ambitions for a new Irish literature and his somewhat harsh feelings about the demise of English poetry are expressed in the last lines of the article he wrote about the Rhymers' Club for *The Boston Pilot*:

> *… for the literature of Ireland is still young, and on all sides of this road is Celtic tradition and Celtic passion crying for singers to give them voice. England is old and her poets must scrape up the crumbs of an almost finished banquet, but Ireland has still full tables.*

On June 13th, 1888, shortly before his twenty-third birthday, Yeats was invited to lecture on 'Sligo Fairies' to the Southwark Irish Literary Club that held its meetings at the Clapham Reform Club. This 'club' was made up of 'young people, clerks, shop-boys, and shop-girls that … got the giggles when any member of the Committee got up to speak'.

Yeats instantly recognised the value of such an organisation both in Ireland and in London and identified the need to revitalise its energy and structure. He invited the club's committee to Bedford Park and proposed a new organisation, the Irish Literary Society, whose inaugural meeting took place in May 1892 at the Caledonian Hotel in The Strand. Coincidentally its first secretary was Evelyn Gleeson, who would later co-found Dun Emer Industries with the two Yeats sisters.

The ILS had soon enrolled every London-Irish author and journalist into its membership, including soon-to-be Irish literary luminaries Douglas Hyde and Charles Gavan Duffy. Though the ILS primarily promoted Irish literature in the English language, it also instituted Irish-language classes at an early stage and brought Irish actors to London to perform plays by Irish writers such as Lady Gregory, Yeats and John Todhunter. In keeping with this desire to promote Irish literature, in 1895 Yeats edited *A Book of Irish Verse*, which contained works by Irish poets ranging from Goldsmith and Thomas Moore to George Russell (Æ), Oscar Wilde and Katharine Tynan Hinkson. At the same time, he was deeply involved with founding a similar organisation in Ireland called the National Literary Society.

* * *

My first meeting with Oscar Wilde was an astonishment. I never before heard a man talking with perfect sentences, as if he had written them all overnight with labour and yet all spontaneous.
– The Trembling of the Veil, 1922

Yeats spent Christmas Day 1888 with Oscar Wilde and his family at the Wildes' home at 34 Tite Street, Chelsea. They had first met when Yeats attended a lecture Wilde gave in Dublin, and got to know each other better through their various literary connections in London as well as the weekly literary gatherings that Wilde's mother, Lady Jane Wilde

'A man talking with perfect sentences': Oscar Wilde

('Speranza'), hosted at her Oakley Street home. Oscar, being ten years older and sympathetic towards the young Yeats, who was at this time twenty-three years old, thought him alone and without family or friend at Christmas, and invited him to dinner with his own family – an invitation which Yeats was delighted to accept.

He lived in a little house at Chelsea that the architect Godwin had decorated with an elegance that owed something to Whistler. There was nothing mediaeval nor Pre-Raphaelite, no cupboard door with figures upon flat gold, no peacock-blue, no dark background ... It was perhaps too perfect in its unity, his past of a few years before had gone too completely, and I remember thinking that the perfect harmony of his life there, with his beautiful wife and his two young children, suggested some deliberate artistic composition.

He commended and dispraised himself during dinner by attributing characteristics like his own to his country: 'We Irish are too poetical to be poets; we are a nation of brilliant failures, but we are the greatest talkers since the Greeks.'

– The Trembling of the Veil, 1922

Wilde and Yeats became closer still over the following years. Wilde read Yeats proofs of some of his own work and positively reviewed some of Yeats's. Throughout Wilde's trial, Yeats stood by him and even gathered letters of support from other Irish writers that he delivered to Wilde's mother's house at Oakley Street.

Lough Gill, Sligo, seen through the hawthorn trees

AFTERWORD

'The work is done,' grown old he thought,
'According to my boyish plan;
Let the fools rage, I swerved in nought,
Something to perfection brought';
But louder sang that ghost, 'What then?'

– from 'What Then?' *(New Poems,* 1938*)*

Throughout his life W.B. Yeats was extremely mobile; during a period when travel was difficult and time-consuming, he became associated with a broad spectrum of locations. He knew London with an intimacy that allowed him to walk its streets, visit its institutions, travel to its suburbs, and know its people with an engaging and culturally entrepreneurial spirit. Similarly, Dublin, the place of his birth and his home for many years, was embraced by him and embraced him in return. It is not only his poetry and plays that stand in testimony to his life there; institutions such as the Abbey Theatre, and, to a lesser extent, Dublin City Gallery: The Hugh Lane are monuments to his vision, energy and perseverance that left indelible marks on the fabric of Irish life.

Yeats's journey took him all around Ireland, and he left his literary footprints as he went; from Dublin to Wicklow to Waterford, where he walked among schoolchildren, to his beloved Galway, where Coole Park and Thoor Ballylee became prominent edifices in his work and life. He acquired a deep knowledge of these places that allowed him to enter the homes of country people and record their tales, and was inspired by them to write about fishermen, horsemen and women, nature, the political environment, and his own emotional world, distilling his observations into their literary essences.

As anyone familiar with Yeats's work knows, his journey begins and ends in Sligo. This is where the magic began, and where, in his father's words, he gave tongue to the sea-cliffs to which he was linked through his colourful ancestry. In Sligo he could place mythologies and legends in real places, and could insert his poet's vision into the wild and rugged landscapes of Ben Bulben, Knocknarea and a host of locations whose names are now synonymous with his own.

But it is not only locus that we associate with Yeats. His works are populated by a vast *dramatis personae* of those whom he met and who inspired him throughout his journey, taking inspiration from them for his philosophy and his work. The poet, statesman, agitator, visionary and lover recorded his encounters with the people he met – eccentric, ordinary writers, painters, actors, revolutionaries – and described them with an honesty that refused to flatter his subjects, his moral and literary courage demanding that he be truthful to his muse and suffer the consequences of that forthrightness. His personal humility as man and poet is evidenced in his love poems, where, in the face of constant rejection by Maud Gonne, he persisted in declaring his love, shaping his rejection into the words we treasure today.

This wandering, restless poet struggled against adversity and resistance to his ideas, while maintaining an unconditional determination to pursue broad artistic goals that impacted not only his own life, but also the cultural and political aspirations of a nation.

REFERENCES

Works by W.B. Yeats

– *Autobiographies*, 1927
Yeats, W.B. *Autobiographies: Reveries over Childhood and Youth; and The Trembling of the Veil*. New York: Macmillan, 1927.

– *The Celtic Twilight*, 1893
Yeats, W.B. *The Celtic Twilight*. London: Lawrence and Bullen, 1893.

– *The Countess Cathleen*, 1892
Yeats, W.B. *The Countess Cathleen and Various Legends and Lyrics*. London: T. Fisher Unwin, 1892.

– *Dramatis Personae*, 1936
Yeats, W.B. *Dramatis Personae*. Dublin: Cuala Press, 1936.

– *Four Years*, 1921
Yeats, W. B. *Four Years*. Dublin: The Cuala Press, 1921.

– *The Green Helmet*, 1910
Yeats, W.B. *The Green Helmet and Other Poems*. Dublin: Cuala Press, 1910.

– *Ideas of Good and Evil*, 1903
Yeats, W.B. *Ideas of Good and Evil*. London: A.H. Bullen, 1903.

– *In the Seven Woods*, 1904
Yeats, W.B. *In the Seven Woods*. Dublin: Dun Emer Press, 1904.

– *Last Poems*, 1939
Yeats, W.B. *Last Poems*. Dublin: Cuala Press, 1939.

– *Michael Robartes and the Dancer*, 1921
Yeats, W.B. *Michael Robartes and the Dancer*. Dublin: Cuala Press, 1921.

– *New Poems*, 1938
Yeats, W.B. *New Poems*. Dublin: Cuala Press, 1938.

– *On the Boiler*, 1938
Yeats, W.B. *On the Boiler*. Dublin: Cuala Press, 1938.

– *Poems*, 1895
Yeats, W.B. *Poems*. London: T. F. Unwin, 1895.

– *Poems Written in Discouragement*, 1913
Yeats, W.B. *Poems Written in Discouragement: 1912–1913*. Dublin: Cuala Press, 1913.

– *Responsibilities*, 1914
Yeats, W.B. *Responsibilities: Poems and a Play*. Dublin: Cuala Press, 1914.

– *Reveries*, 1915
Yeats, W.B. *Reveries over Childhood and Youth*. Dublin: Cuala Press, 1915.

– *The Secret Rose*, 1897
Yeats, W.B. *The Secret Rose*. London: Lawrence & Bullen, 1897.

– *The Tower*, 1928
Yeats, W.B. *The Tower*. London: Macmillan, 1928.

– *The Trembling of the Veil*, 1922
Yeats, W.B. *The Trembling of the Veil*. London: T.W. Laurie, 1922.

– *A Vision*, 1925
Yeats, W.B. *A Vision*. London: Macmillan, 1925.

– *The Wanderings of Oisin and Other Poems*, 1889

Yeats, W.B. *The Wanderings of Oisin and Other Poems*. London: Kegan Paul Trench & Co., 1889.

– *The Wild Swans at Coole*, 1919

Yeats, W.B. *The Wild Swans at Coole*. London: Macmillan, 1919.

– *The Wind Among the Reeds*, 1899

Yeats, W.B. *The Wind Among the Reeds*. London: Elkin Mathews, 1899.

– *The Winding Stair*, 1933

Yeats, W.B. *The Winding Stair and Other Poems*. London: Macmillan, 1933.

* * *

Collections and other writings

– *The Boston Pilot*, 1890

W.B. Yeats's review of *A Sicilian Idyll* in *The Boston Pilot*, June 1890.

– *The Boston Pilot*, 1892

Yeats, W.B. 'Maud Gonne', published in *The Boston Pilot*, July 1892.

– *Collected Works IX*, 2010

Frayne, John P. and Marchaterre, Madeleine (eds). *The Collected Works of W.B. Yeats Volume IX: Early Articles and Reviews*. New York: Scribner, 2010.

– *Letters Volume 1*, 1889

Kelly, John (ed.), *The Collected Letters of W.B. Yeats Volume 1: 1865–1895*. Oxford: Clarendon Press, 1986.

– *Letters*, 1954

Wade, Allan (ed.). *The Letters of W.B. Yeats*. London: Hart-Davis, 1954.

– *Memoirs*, 1972
Donoghue, Denis (ed.). *Memoirs of W.B. Yeats: Autobiography and First Draft Journal*. London: Macmillan, 1972.

– 'The Rhymers' Club', published in *The Boston Pilot*. Quoted in *Letters to the New Island*, 1989
Yeats, W.B. 'The Rhymers' Club', published in *The Boston Pilot*, April 1892. Quoted in: Bornstein, George and Witemeyer, Hugh (eds). *Letters to the New Island*. London: Palgrave Macmillan, 1989.

– *The Senate Speeches*, 1960
Pearce, Donald R. (ed.). *The Senate Speeches of W.B. Yeats*. Bloomington: Indiana University Press, 1960.

– *W. B. Yeats and George Yeats: The Letters*, 2011
Saddlemyer, Ann (ed.), *W. B. Yeats and George Yeats: The Letter*s. Oxford: Oxford University Press, 2011.

* * *

Works by others

– Donald T. Torchiana, 1965
Torchiana, Donald T. '"Among School Children" and the Education of the Irish Spirit', quoted in *In Excited Reverie*, A. Norman Jeffares and K.G.W. Cross (eds). London: Macmillan, 1965.

– *Early Memories* by John Butler Yeats, 1923
Yeats, John Butler. *Early Memories: Some Chapters of Autobiography.* Dublin: Cuala Press, 1923.

– *The Fays of the Abbey Theatre* by W.G. Fay & Catherine Carswell, 1935
Fay, W.G. and Carswell, Catherine, *The Fays of the Abbey Theatre*. New

York: Harcourt, Brace and Company, 1935.

– *J.B. Yeats: Letters to His Son*, 1944
Hone, Joseph (ed.). *J.B. Yeats: Letters to His Son W.B. Yeats and Others.*
London: Faber & Faber, 1944.

– Macken, 1939
Extracted from 'W.B. Yeats, John O'Leary and the Contemporary Club' by
Mary L. Macken. *Studies: An Irish Quarterly Review* Vol. 28, No. 109, 1939.

– 'Memories of Yeats', 1939
Mary Colum, 'Memories of Yeats', *Saturday Review of Literature*, 25
February 1939.

– *Our Irish Theatre* by Lady Gregory, 1913
Gregory, Lady Augusta Persse. *Our Irish Theatre: A Chapter of
Autobiography.* New York: The Knickerbocker Press, 1913.

– *Poet Lore*, 1906
Extracted from *Poet Lore* (Boston) XVII, No. 2, June 1906.

– *Prodigal Father*, 1978
Murphy, William M. *Prodigal Father: The Life of John Butler Yeats*. Ithaca
and London: Cornell University Press, 1978.

– *Reminiscences* by Katharine Tynan, 1913
Tynan, Katharine. *Twenty-Five Years: Reminiscences*. London: Smith, Elder
and Co., 1913.

– *Scattering Branches*, 1940
Gwynn, Stephen (ed.). *Scattering Branches: Tributes to the Memory of W.B.
Yeats*. London: Macmillan, 1940.

– *The Second Book of the Rhymers' Club*, 1894

Rhymers' Club (London, England). *The Second Book of the Rhymers' Club*. London: Elkin Mathews & John Lane, 1894.

– *A Servant of the Queen* by Maud Gonne, 1950

Gonne, Maud. *A Servant of the Queen: Her Own Story*. Dublin: Golden Eagle Books, 1950.

– *T.P.'s Weekly*, 1912

Extracted from *T.P.'s Weekly* (London) XIX, No. 500, 7 June 1912.

ILLUSTRATIONS

The author and publisher thank the following for permission to use photographs and illustrative material: Pages 8, 11, 12–13, 14–15, 21, 25, 28–29, 34, 61, 78, 83, 88–89, 90, 98–99, 104, 124, 126, 134, 137, 146–147, 154–155, 156–157, 160–161, 167, 184, 190–191, 192, 227 (both), 238, 240–241 and 242 courtesy of Shutterstock. Pages 16 (top), 96, 107, 115, 119, 120, 128–129 and 153 courtesy of Sean Kennedy. Pages 17 (bottom), 32, 75, 84, 95, 205, 219 and 229 courtesy of the National Library of Ireland. Pages 38, 42, 49, 81 and 209 courtesy of Dublin City Library and Archives. Pages 50, 63, 66, 71, 72, 109, 113, 132, 139, 150, 158, 170, 176, 181, 187, 189, 194, 197, 200, 211, 220, 222, 225 and 232: photos in the public domain. Page 54: John Singer Sargent, 'Portrait of Sir Hugh Lane', 1906, Reg.132 © Dublin City Gallery, The Hugh Lane. Page 142 courtesy of Richard Mills. Page 164 photograph taken by W.E. Bailey, courtesy of Colin Smythe. Page 166 courtesy of James Fraher. Page 216 © Private Collection / Bridgeman Images. If any involuntary infringement of copyright has occurred, sincere apologies are offered, and the owners of such copyright are requested to contact the publisher.

INDEX